Writing for Social Scientists

Chicago Guides
to *Writing*, Editing,
and Publishing

How to Start and
Finish Your Thesis,
Book, or Article

THIRD EDITION

Howard S. Becker

with a chapter by

PAMELA RICHARDS

The University of Chicago Press

Chicago and London

WRITING for SOCIAL SCIENTISTS

The University of Chicago Press, Chicago 60637

The University of Chicago Press, Ltd., London

Published 2020

Printed in the United States of America

29 28 27 26 25 24 23 22 21 20   1 2 3 4 5

ISBN-13: 978-0-226-68363-8 (cloth)

ISBN-13: 978-0-226-64393-9 (paper)

ISBN-13: 978-0-226-64409-7 (ebook)

DOI: https://doi.org/10.7208/chicago/9780226644097.001.0001

Library of Congress Cataloging-in-Publication Data

Names: Becker, Howard Saul, 1928– author. | Richards, Pamela. Risk.

Title: Writing for social scientists : how to start and finish your thesis, book, or article / Howard S. Becker ; with a chapter by Pamela Richards.

Other titles: Chicago guides to writing, editing, and publishing.

Description: Third edition. | Chicago ; London : The University of Chicago Press, 2020. | Series: Chicago guides to writing, editing, and publishing | Includes bibliographical references and index.

Identifiers: LCCN 2019031496 | ISBN 9780226683638 (cloth) | ISBN 9780226643939 (paperback) | ISBN 9780226644097 (ebook)

Subjects: LCSH: Social sciences—Authorship. | Sociology—Authorship. | Academic writing. | Communication in the social sciences.

Classification: LCC H61.8 .B43 2020 | DDC 808.06/63—dc23

LC record available at https://lccn.loc.gov/2019031496

♾ This paper meets the requirements of ANSI/NISO Z39.48-1992 (Permanence of Paper).

This book is dedicated to the memory of
DOUGLAS MITCHELL,
much beloved and admired longtime sociology editor at
the University of Chicago Press, who had an eye for
good thinking and good writing.

Contents

Preface to the Third Edition

I wrote the first version of this book in the early 1980s. It came very easily. I'd been teaching writing to graduate students for a few years, and that experience had given me a lot to think about and a lot of stories to tell. The stories generally had a point, a small lesson about why we have the problems we do in writing, or a possibility of avoiding those problems, or a way of thinking that would make the problem seem less problematic. After the first chapter appeared in a journal, and excited some discussion, I saw that I had a beginning, and the rest of the book almost wrote itself and was soon published.

I didn't, despite the title of the first chapter, rewrite a freshman English text for graduate students. I can't compete with the standard works in English composition, whose authors know more about grammar, syntax, and the other classic topics than I do, and I haven't tried. Some of these matters appear briefly, largely because I am pretty sure that graduate students and young professionals in sociology and related disciplines won't search out or heed advice from outside their own field. They ought to. But if writing about society will improve only when sociologists study grammar and syntax seriously, then it never will.

Further, problems of style and diction invariably involve matters of substance. Bad sociological writing, as I'll explain later, can't be separated from the theoretical problems of the discipline. In the end, the way people write grows out of the social situations they write in. So we have to see (this summarizes the book's perspective) how social organization creates the classic problems of scholarly writing: style, organization, and the rest. Instead of trying to write a freshman English book I'm not competent to write, then, I tried to create an analysis addressing the specific problems of writing about society by approaching the technical problems (those other authors write about) sociologically. I deal specifically with scholarly, and especially sociological, writing and set its problems in the context of scholarly work. (Most of Umberto Eco's excellent book [2015] on how to write a dissertation concerns the politics and logistics of the process—choosing dissertation advisers, for instance, or which libraries to look for sources in—rather than the actual writing.)

I have, immodestly, written personally and autobiographically, because I think students have trouble imagining writing as a real activity real people do. Students don't think of books as someone's work. Even graduate students, who are much closer to their instructors, seldom see anyone actually writing, rarely see working drafts, or writing that isn't ready for publication. It was and usually still is a mystery to them. I want to remove the mystery and let them see that the work they read is made by people who have the same difficulties they do. My prose is not exemplary but, since I know what went into its making, I can discuss why I wrote it that way, what problems I had, and how I found solutions. I can't do that with anyone else's work. Since I have been producing sociological writing for a long time, many students and professionals have read some of it, and readers of this book tell me that it's useful to know that those pieces troubled and confused me just as their work bothers them. So I've devoted a chapter to my own experiences as a writer.

A lot of people found the book useful. Departments occasionally bought copies for all their incoming graduate students (I guess because faculty hoped it might counter their fears and anxieties). Students who felt it had helped them recommended or even gave it to their buddies.

But nothing prepared me for the steady stream of mail from readers who found the book helpful. Several even told me the book had saved their lives—less a testimony to the book as therapy than a reflection of the seriousness of the trouble writing failure could get people into. Many told me that they had given the book to friends who were having serious problems. It's not surprising, given the degree to which our fate in the academic environments we write in as students, teachers, and researchers hangs on our ability to turn out acceptable prose on demand.

When you can't do that, your confidence goes down, which makes it harder to get the next writing chore done, and before you know it you can't see a way out. So the book, suggesting new ways of looking at these dilemmas, gave people hope and helped at least some of them get the spiral going in the other direction.

I wasn't prepared, either, for the thank yous from people in fields far from my own discipline of sociology. Much of the analysis in the book is straightforwardly and unapologetically sociological, finding the roots of writing problems and the possibilities of their solution in social organization. Many of the specific problems that produce the convoluted, almost unreadable prose readers complain of as "academic" seemed to me then to arise from such specifically sociological worries as wanting to avoid making causal statements when you knew you didn't have the proof that kind of talk required (that's taken up in chapter 1). I found out that people in many other fields—art history, communications, literature, and so on (it was a long and surprising list)—had similar difficulties. I hadn't had them in mind, but the shoe seemed to fit.

Since I last revised this book, the environment students and teachers live and work in has changed a lot. Students are still, of course, beginners who don't know how to do the writing they must do.

But personal computers began arriving in universities at roughly the same time as I began my experiments teaching writing, and they changed the environment in ways I never imagined they would. And so, as C. Wright Mills would surely have predicted, the changes in academia that came with them have changed what's problematic for the people who work there, adding possibilities no one had anticipated but that various players in the university environment have been able to exploit in unexpected ways. The basic problems the book discusses are still there but new dangers and possibilities have now added new considerations to the calculations writers have to make (and so, to what I had to write about).

I have abandoned listing all the people whose advice, criticisms, and encouragement helped me finish this work and improve it. There are just too many, and the number dilutes the meaning of the acknowledgement. I do owe special thanks to Rosanna Hertz for writing the letter that prompted the chapter on "Persona and Authority" and for letting me quote from it so extensively. A letter Pamela Richards wrote to me about risk was so complete as it stood that I asked her if she would let it appear in this volume under her name. I'm glad she agreed; I couldn't have said it half so well. And I must gratefully acknowledge that chapter 1 originally appeared, in a slightly different form, in the *Sociological Quarterly* 24 (Autumn 1983): 575–88, and is reprinted here with the permission of the Midwest Sociological Society, and that the short article called "Long-Term Changes in the Character of the Sociological Discipline: A Note on the Length of Titles of Articles Submitted to the *American Sociological Review* during the Year 2002" first appeared in 2003 in the *American Sociological Review* 68: iii–v, and is here reprinted in chapter 10, with permission of the American Sociological Society.

I know that manuscripts don't somehow magically turn into printed and bound books. And so I want to register my gratitude to the people at the University of Chicago Press for everything they did to make that magic happen. Douglas Mitchell was the acquisitions editor who saw merit in it and started the ball rolling, and kept it rolling all these years. Mary Laur, editor of the series in which it appears, oversaw this latest version. Susan Karani did the final copyediting. And many other people, most of whose names I don't think I ever knew, chose typefaces and page layouts that made it so easy to read. My deepest thanks to all of them.

Finally, Dianne Hagaman has stuck with me through this revision, as she has through everything else for all these years. She's given me the benefit of her experience and judgment, which are reflected in everything you'll read in what follows.

Howard S. Becker
San Francisco, 2019

1 : Freshman English for Graduate Students

I taught a seminar on writing for graduate students (and others) several times over the course of my professorial career. That required a certain amount of chutzpah. After all, to teach a topic suggests that you know something about it. Writing professionally, as a sociologist, for many years gave me some claim to that knowledge. In addition, several teachers and colleagues had not only criticized my prose, but had given me innumerable lessons meant to improve it. On the other hand, "everyone knew" that sociologists wrote very badly, so that literary types could make jokes about bad writing just by saying "sociology," the way old-time comedians used to get a laugh just by saying "Peoria" or "Cucamonga." The experience and lessons haven't saved me from the faults I still share with those colleagues.

Nevertheless, sometime in the 1970s, I took the chance, driven to it by stories of the chronic problems students and fellow sociologists had with writing. I listed the course.

The turnout for the first class surprised me. Not only did ten or twelve graduate students sign up, but the class also contained a couple of post-PhD researchers and even a few of my younger faculty colleagues, and that pattern of enrollment continued in succeeding years. Their worries and troubles with writing overshadowed the fear of embarrassing themselves by going back to school.

My chutzpah went beyond teaching a course whose subject I was no master of. I didn't even prepare for the class, because (being a sociologist, not a teacher of composition) I had no idea how to teach it. So I walked in the first day not knowing what I would do. After a few fumbling preliminary remarks, I had a flash. I had been reading the *Paris Review Interviews with Writers* for years and had always had a slightly prurient interest in what the interviewed authors shamelessly revealed about their writing habits. So I turned to a former graduate student and old friend sitting on my left and said, "Louise, how do you write?" I explained that I was not interested in any fancy talk about scholarly preparations but, rather, in the nitty-gritty details, whether she typed or wrote in longhand (this was in the days before personal computers), used any special kind of paper, or worked at any special time of day. I didn't know what she would say.

The hunch paid off. She gave, more or less unselfconsciously, a lengthy account of an elaborate routine which had to be done just so. Although she was not embarrassed by what she described, others squirmed a little as she explained that she could only write on yellow, ruled, legal-size pads using a green felt-tip pen, that she had to clean the house first (that turned out to be a common preliminary for women but not for men, who were more likely to sharpen twenty pencils), that she could only write between such and such hours, and so on.

I knew I was on to something and went on to the next victim. A little more reluctantly, he described his equally peculiar habits.

The third one said he was sorry but he'd like to pass his turn. I didn't allow that. He had a good reason, as it turned out. They all did. By then they could see that what people were describing was something quite shameful, nothing you wanted to talk about in front of twenty other people. I was relentless, making everyone tell all and not sparing myself.

This exercise created great tension, but also a lot of joking, enormous interest, and eventually a surprising relaxation. I pointed out that they all were relieved, and ought to be, because, while their worst fears were true—they really were crazy—they were no crazier than anyone else. It was a common disease. Just as people feel relieved to discover that some frightening physical symptoms they've been hiding are just something that is "going around," knowing that others had crazy writing habits should have been, and clearly was, a good thing.

I went on with my interpretation. From one point of view, my fellow participants were describing neurotic symptoms. Viewed sociologically, however, those symptoms were magical rituals. According to the anthropologist Bronislaw Malinowski (1948, 25–36), people perform such rituals to influence the result of some process over which they think they have no rational means of control. He described the phenomenon as he observed it among the Trobriand Islanders:

> Thus in canoe building empirical knowledge of material, of technology, and of certain principles of stability and hydrodynamics, function in company and in close association with magic, each yet uncontaminated by the other.
>
> For example, they understand perfectly well that the wider the span of the outrigger the greater the stability yet the smaller the resistance against strain. They can clearly explain why they have to give this span a certain traditional width, measured in fractions of the length of the dugout. They can also explain, in rudimentary but clearly mechanical terms, how they have to behave in a sudden gale, why the outrigger must always be on the weather side, why the one

type of canoe can and the other cannot beat. They have, in fact, a whole system of principles of sailing, embodied in a complex and rich terminology, traditionally handed on and obeyed as rationally and consistently as is modern science by modern sailors. . . .

But even with all their systematic knowledge, methodically applied, they are still at the mercy of powerful and incalculable tides, sudden gales during the monsoon season and unknown reefs. And here comes in their magic, performed over the canoe during its construction, carried out at the beginning and in the course of expeditions and resorted to in moments of real danger. (30–31)

Just like the Trobriand sailors, sociologists who couldn't handle the dangers of writing in a rational way used magical charms to dispel anxiety, though without really affecting the result.

So I asked the class: What are you so afraid of not being able to control rationally that you have to use all these magical spells and rituals? I'm no Freudian, but I did think they would resist answering the question. They didn't. On the contrary, they spoke easily and at length. They feared, to summarize the long discussion that followed, two things. They were afraid that they would not be able to organize their thoughts, that writing would be a big, confusing chaos that would drive them mad. And they spoke feelingly about a second fear: that what they wrote would be "wrong" and that (unspecified) people would laugh at them. That seemed to account for more of the ritual. A second person who wrote on legal-sized yellow ruled tablets and always started on the second page. Why? Well, she said, if anyone walked by, you could pull down the top sheet and cover what you had been writing so the passerby couldn't see. (If she had been writing on a laptop, she could have gotten the same result by switching to another screen.)

Many of the rituals ensured that what was written could not be taken for a "finished" product, so no one could laugh at it. The excuse was built in. I think that's why even writers who type well sometimes still use such time-wasting methods as longhand. Anything written in longhand is clearly not yet done and so cannot be criticized as though it were. You can keep people from taking your writing as a serious expression of your abilities even more surely, however, by not writing at all. No one can read what has never been put on down in a visually accessible form.

Something important had happened in that class. As I also pointed out to them that first day, they had all told something quite shameful about themselves, and no one had died. (Here what had happened resembled what might have happened in some kinds of group therapy, which relied on people revealing their psyches or bodies in public and discovering that the revelation, similarly, does not kill.) It surprised me that people in this class, many of whom knew each other quite well, knew nothing at all about each other's work habits and, in fact, had hardly ever seen each other's writing. I decided to do something about that.

I had originally told prospective class members that the class would emphasize, instead of write, edit, and rewrite. Therefore I made the price of admission to the class an already written paper on which they would now practice rewriting. Before tackling these papers, however, I decided to show them what it meant to rewrite and edit. A colleague lent me a rough second draft of a paper she was working on. I distributed her three- or four-page "methods section" at the beginning of the second class, and we spent three hours rewriting it.

Sociologists habitually use twenty words where two will do, and we spent most of that afternoon cutting excess words. I used a trick I had often used in private lessons. With my pencil poised over a word or clause, I asked, "Does this need to be here? If not, I'm taking it out." I insisted that we must not, in making any change, lose the slightest nuance of the author's thought. (I had in mind here the rules C. Wright Mills followed in his masterful "translation" of passages from Talcott Parsons [Mills 1959, 27–31.]) If no one defended the word or phrase, I took it out. I changed passive to active constructions, combined sentences, took long sentences apart—all the things these students might

5

well have once learned to do in freshman composition. At the end of three hours, we had reduced four pages to three-quarters of a page without losing any nuance or essential detail.

We worked on one long sentence—which considered the possible implications of what the paper had so far said—for quite a while, removing words and phrases until it was a quarter as long as it had been. I finally suggested (mischievously, but they weren't sure of that) that we cut the whole thing and just say, "So what?" Someone finally broke the stunned silence: "You could get away with that, but we couldn't." So we talked about tone, concluding that I couldn't get away with it either, unless I had properly prepared for that sort of tone, and it was appropriate to the occasion.

The students felt very sorry for my colleague who had donated the pages we did this surgery on. They thought she had been humiliated, that it was lucky she hadn't been there to die of shame. In empathizing that way, they relied on their own unprofessional feelings, not realizing that people who write professionally, and write a lot, routinely rewrite as we just had. I wanted them to believe that this was not unusual and that they should expect to rewrite a lot, so I told them (truthfully) that I habitually rewrote manuscripts eight to ten times before publication (although not before giving them to my friends to read). Since, as I'll explain later, they thought that "good writers" (people like their teachers) got everything right the first time, that shocked them.

This exercise had several results. The students were exhausted, never having spent so much time on or looked so closely at one piece of writing, never having imagined that anyone could spend so much time on such a job. They had seen and experimented with a number of standard editorial devices. But the most important result came at the end of the afternoon when, exhaustedly, one student—that wonderful student who says what others are thinking but know better than to say—said, "Gee, Howie, when you say it this way, it looks like something anybody could say." You bet.

We talked about that. Was it what you said that was sociological, or was it the way you said it? Mind you, we had not replaced any technical sociological language. That had not been the problem (it almost never is). We had replaced redundancies, "fancy writing," pompous phrases (for instance, my personal bête noire, "the way in which," for which a plain "how" can usually be substituted without losing anything but pretentiousness)—anything that could be simplified without damage to the thought. We decided that authors tried to give substance and weight to what they wrote by sounding academic, even at the expense of their real meaning.

We discovered some other things that interminable afternoon. Some of those long, redundant expressions couldn't be replaced because they had no underlying sense to replace. They were placeholders, marking a spot where the author should have said something plainer but had at the moment nothing plain to say. These spots nevertheless had to be filled because otherwise the author would only have half a sentence. Writers did not use these meaningless phrases and sentences randomly or simply because they had bad writing habits. Certain situations evoked meaningless placeholders.

Writers routinely use meaningless expressions to cover up two kinds of problems. Both kinds of problems reflect serious dilemmas of sociological theory. One problem has to do with what is usually called "agency": who did it? Who did the things your sentence alleges were done? Sociologists often prefer locutions that leave the answer to that question unclear, largely because many of their theories don't tell them who is doing what. In many sociological theories, things just happen without anyone doing them. It's hard to find a subject for a sentence when "larger social forces" or "inexorable social processes" are at work. Avoiding saying who did it produces two characteristic faults of sociological writing: the habitual use of passive constructions and abstract nouns.

If you say, for example, that "deviants were labeled," you don't have to say who labeled them. That is a theoretical error, not just bad writing. A major point of the labeling theory of deviance (outlined in Becker 2018) is precisely that *someone* labels the person deviant, someone with the power to do it and good reasons for wanting to. If you leave those actors out, you misstate the theory, both in letter and spirit. Yet it is a common locution. Sociologists commit similar theoretical errors when they say that society does this or that or that culture makes people do things, and sociologists do write that way all the time.

Sociologists' inability or unwillingness to make causal statements similarly leads to bad writing. David Hume's *Essay Concerning Human Understanding* makes us all nervous about claiming to demonstrate causal connections and, though few sociologists are as skeptical as Hume, most understand that despite the efforts of John Stuart Mill, the Vienna Circle, and all the rest, they run serious scholarly risks when they allege that A causes B. Sociologists have many ways of describing how elements covary, most of them vacuous expressions hinting at what we would like, but don't dare, to say. Since we are afraid to say that A causes B, we say, "There is a tendency for them to covary" or "They seem to be associated."

The reasons for doing this bring us back to the rituals of writing. We write that way because we fear that others will catch us in obvious errors if we do anything else, and laugh at us. Better to say something innocuous but safe than something bold you might not be able to defend against criticism. Mind you, it wouldn't be objectionable to say, "A varies with B," if that's what you really want to say, and it is certainly reasonable to say, "I think A causes B and my data support that by showing that they covary." But many people use such expressions to hint at stronger assertions they just don't want to take the rap for. They want to discover causes, because causes are scientifically interesting, but don't want the philosophical responsibility.

Every teacher of English composition and every guide to writing criticizes passive constructions, abstract nouns, and most of the other faults I mentioned. I did not invent these standards. In fact, I learned them in composition classes myself. Although the standards are thus independent of any particular school of thought, I believe that my preference for clarity and directness also has roots in the symbolic interactionist tradition of sociology, which focuses on real actors in real situations. My Brazilian colleague Gilberto Velho used to insist that these are ethnocentric standards, strongly favored in the Anglo-American tradition of plain speaking, but having no more warrant than the more flowery, indirect style of some European traditions. I think that's wrong, since some of the best writers in other languages also use a direct style.

Similarly, Michael Schudson once asked me, not unreasonably, how someone ought to write who believes that structures—capitalist relations of production, for instance—cause social phenomena. Should such a theorist use passive constructions to indicate the passivity of the human actors involved? That question requires two answers. The simpler is that few serious theories of society leave no room for human agency. More importantly, passive constructions even hide the agency attributed to systems and structures. Suppose a system does the labeling of deviants. Saying "deviants are labeled" covers that up too.

Much of what we removed from my colleague's paper in class consisted of what I named, for class purposes (with Wayne Booth's criticism of academic "Greek-fed, polysyllabic bullshit" (Booth 1979, 277) as legitimating precedent), "bullshit qualifications," vague phrases expressing a general readiness to abandon the point being made if anyone objects: "A tends to be related to B," "A might possibly tend to be related to B under some conditions," and similar cowardly qualifiers. A real qualification says that A is related to B except under certain specified circumstances: I always shop for groceries at the Safeway unless it's closed; the positive relationship between income and education is stronger in white populations than in black populations. But the students, like other sociologists, habitually used less specific qualifications. They wanted to say that the relationship existed, but knew that someone would, sooner or later, find an exception. The nonspecific, ritual qualifier gave them an all-purpose loophole. If attacked, they could say they never said it was always true. Bullshit qualifications, making your statements fuzzy, ignore the philosophical and methodological tradition which holds that making generalizations in a strong universal form identifies the kind of negative evidence that could be used to improve them.

As I asked people in the class about why they wrote the way they did, I learned that they had picked up many of their habits in high school and solidified them in college. What they had learned to write were then called *term papers* and are now often called *research papers*. You write such a paper by doing whatever reading or research is required throughout the term and working out the paper in your head as you go along. But you write only one draft, perhaps after making an outline, usually the night before handing it in. Like a Japanese brush painting, you do it, and either it's okay or it isn't. College students have no time for rewriting, since they often have several papers due at the same time. The method usually works well for undergraduates. Some become very adept at the format and turn out creditable, highly polished papers, working on them in their heads as they walk around campus, putting the words on paper as the assignments come due. Teachers know all this. If they aren't aware of the mechanics, they know the typical results and don't expect papers more coherent or highly polished than such a method can produce.

Students who habitually work that way understandably worry about the draft they produce. They know it could be better but is not going to be. Whatever they put down is *it*. As long as that document is kept confidential, in the conventionally private teacher-undergraduate relationship, it won't embarrass the author too much.

But the social organization of writing and reputation changes in graduate school. Teachers talk about your papers, for good or bad, to their colleagues and to other students. With luck, the papers grow into qualifying papers or dissertations, read by several faculty members.

Graduate students also write longer papers than undergraduates do. Students expert at the one-shot term paper cannot hold a longer paper in their heads so easily. That's when they start losing their ability to write. They cannot produce a one-draft paper and be confident that it will not provoke ridicule and criticism. So they don't write.

I didn't tell the students all this during the first class sessions, though I eventually did. Instead, I gave assignments that would get them to give up the one-draft method of producing papers. They might then find alternate routines that were less painful and equally effective in earning academic rewards. A few adventurous students in each of the several classes I taught trusted me enough to go along with these experiments. My reputation for not being fierce weakened the traditional student fear of professors, and those who had taken other classes with me trusted my eccentricities. Teachers who lack that advantage might have more trouble using some of these tricks.

I told students that it didn't make much difference what they wrote in a first draft because they could always change it. Since what they put on a piece of paper was not necessarily final, they needn't worry so much about what they wrote. The only version that mattered was the last one. They had gotten a glimpse of how things could be changed and I promised to show them more.

Our classroom editing and my interpretation of it sobered the students. I asked them to bring the papers I had required as a prerequisite for admission to the class (but had not yet collected) to the next session. (Some students balked at this. The second year I taught the course, one said she wasn't going to bring a paper because she didn't have one. I got angry: "Anyone who has been going to school as long as you have has plenty of papers. Bring one." Then the real reason came out: "I don't have one that's good enough." I insisted and she gave in. After all, I *was* the teacher.) After collecting the papers and shuffling them thoroughly, I passed them out again, making sure that no one got his or her own. I asked them to edit the papers thoroughly. The next week they returned them to their authors. Students sat soberly, looking to see what had been done. Plenty, was the answer. There was red ink everywhere.

I asked them how they liked editing someone else's paper. They spoke at length, angrily. They had been surprised by how much work there was to do, at how many silly mistakes people made. After an hour of complaining, I asked them how they liked having their papers edited. Again they were upset, but this time they complained that the person who read their paper lacked compassion, couldn't see what they had meant, had changed their text to say things they hadn't intended at all. The smarter ones soon realized that they were talking about themselves, and the group fell silent as that sank in. I said it was a lesson they ought to think about, and that now they could see that they had to write so that well-meaning editors—and they had to assume their colleagues were well-meaning—could not mistake their meaning. Editors and colleagues would often rewrite their work, I told them, and they better get used to it and not let their feelings be hurt by such experiences. They should try instead to write so clearly that no one could misunderstand and make changes they didn't like.

Then I said that they could really start by writing almost anything, any kind of a rough draft, no matter how crude or confused, and make something good out of it. To prove it, I had to get someone to produce a first, uncensored draft, some ideas written with little care and no corrections. I explained that such a draft would help them find out what they might have to say.

This was one of the places where I invented what I did not know was likewise being developed by people in composition theory and elsewhere. Linda Flower (1979, 36), for instance, describes and analyzes the same procedure as "Writer-Based prose," which "allows the writer freedom to generate a breadth of information and a variety of alternative relationships before locking himself or herself into a premature formulation." Years later I read Anne Lamott's *Bird by Bird* (1994) and its strong recommendation of writing "shitty first drafts" as a way to get any writing project started.

It took some work to find someone who would try such a risky process. I distributed copies of the resulting document to the class. The person who contributed the piece made some nervous self-deprecating jokes about putting herself in jeopardy by allowing people to see it. To her surprise, what she had written amazed her classmates. They could see that it was mixed up and written badly, but they could also see, and said, that she had some really interesting ideas there that could be developed. They also openly admired her courage. (Other brave students had the same effect on their peers in succeeding years.)

This draft showed the author approaching her subject circuitously, not sure of what she wanted to say, saying the same thing in several different ways. Comparing the versions made it easy to see the idea she had been circling around and to formulate it more concisely. We found three or four ideas to work with that way and could see, or sense, some connections between them. We agreed that the way to work with such a draft was to take notes on it, see what it contained, and then make an outline for another draft. Why bother avoiding redundancy or any of the other faults we had worked so hard to eliminate the week before, since it would be easy to get rid of them, using those newly learned skills, later? Worrying about those faults might slow you down, keep you from saying something in one of the ways that would give you the clue you needed. Better to edit afterward, rather than as you went. The students began to see that writing need not be a one-shot, all-or-nothing venture. It could have stages, each with its own criteria of excellence (as Flower and others could have told them, but perhaps it was better for them to discover it in their own experience). An insistence on clarity and polish appropriate to a late version was entirely inappropriate to earlier ones meant to get the ideas on paper. In coming to these conclusions, they replicated some of Flower's results and began to understand that worrying about rules of writing too early in the process could keep them from saying what they actually had to say.

I don't want to exaggerate. My students did not throw away their crutches and start dancing. But they saw that there were ways out of their troubles, which was all I'd hoped for. Knowing what was possible, they could try it. Just knowing wasn't enough, of course. They had to use these devices, make them part of their writing routine, perhaps replacing some of the magical elements we had discussed.

We did a number of other things in the seminar. We discussed rhetoric, reading Gusfield (1981) on the rhetoric of social science, and Orwell's "Politics and the English Language" (1954). Surprisingly, to me, Gusfield the sociologist had a stronger impact than Orwell the writer. He showed how writers in the students' own field manipulated stylistic devices to sound "scientific," particularly noting how passive constructions could produce a facade of impersonality the investigator could hide behind. We talked about scientific writing as a form of rhetoric, meant to persuade, and which forms of persuasion the scientific community considered acceptable or not. I insisted on the rhetorical nature of scientific writing, although the students believed, with many of their elders, that some ways of writing illegitimately attempt to persuade while others just presented the facts and let them speak for themselves. (Sociologists of science and students of rhetoric have written extensively on this point. See, especially, Bazerman 1981, and Latour and Bastide 1983, and the accompanying bibliography.)

That student I was so fond of helped me out again here. After we had discussed the rhetoric of science at length, he said, "Okay, Howie, I know you never like to tell us what to do, but are you going to tell us or not?" "Tell you what?" "How to write without using rhetoric!" As before, everyone had been hoping that I would reveal that secret. Just hearing it said aloud confirmed their worst fears. They couldn't write without using rhetoric—no one can—and so they couldn't evade questions of style.

During several years of teaching the course, I developed a theory of writing which describes the process that produces both the writing people do and the difficulties they have doing it. (The theory, in a more general form, appears in *Art Worlds* [Becker 1982a], as a theory of the making of artworks of all kinds. Though it grows out of a sociological social psychology quite different from the cognitive psychology dominating work in composition theory, my notions resembled those of Flower and Hayes and their colleagues.) Any work's eventual form results from all the choices made by all the people involved in producing it. When we write, we constantly make such choices as to which idea to take up and when; what words to use, in what order, to express it, what examples to give to make our meaning clearer. Of course, writing actually follows an even lengthier process of absorbing and developing ideas, similarly preceded by a process of absorbing impressions and sorting them out. Each choice shapes the result.

If that is a reasonable analysis, we kid ourselves when we think, sitting down to write, that we are composing freshly and can write anything at all. Our earlier choices—to look at it this way, to think about this example in developing our ideas, to use this way of gathering and storing data, to read this novel or watch that television program—rule out what we might otherwise have chosen. Every time we answer a question about our work and what we have been finding or thinking, our choice of words affects the way we describe it the next time, perhaps when we are writing notes or making outlines.

Most of the students had a more conventional view, embodied in the folk maxim that if you think clearly, you will write clearly. They thought they had to work everything out before they wrote Word One, having first assembled all their impressions, ideas, and data and explicitly decided every important question of theory and fact. Otherwise, they might get it wrong. They acted the belief out ritually by not beginning to write until they had every book and note they might possibly need piled up on their desks. They further thought they had a free choice in most of these matters, which led to remarks like "I think I'll use Durkheim for my theory section," as if they hadn't already decided the theoretical issues that invoking Durkheim (or Weber or Marx) had suggested long before, in the way they had done their work. (Scholars in other fields will know which Great Names to substitute here.)

My theory leads to the opposite view: you have already made many choices when you sit down to write, but probably don't know what they were. That leads, naturally, to some confusion, to a mixed-up early draft. But a mixed-up draft is no cause for shame. Rather, it shows you what your earlier choices were, what ideas, theoretical viewpoints, and conclusions you had already committed yourself to before you began writing. Knowing that you will write many more drafts, you know that you need not worry about this one's crudeness and lack of coherence. This one is for discovery, not for presentation (the distinction is C. Wright Mills's [1959, 222], following Reichenbach).

Writing an early rough draft, then, shows you all the earlier decisions that now shape what you can write. You can't "use" Marx if Durkheim's ideas shaped your thinking. You can't write about what the data you gathered don't tell you about, or your method of storing them doesn't let you use them for. You see what you have and don't have, what you have already done and already know, and what's left to do. You see that the only job left—even though you have just begun to write—is to make it all clearer. The rough draft shows you what needs to be made clearer; the skills of rewriting and editing let you do it.

It's not that easy, of course. The next choices, made in editing and rewriting, also shape the result. You can no longer do anything you want, but there are plenty of choices left. These further questions of language, organization, and tone often give authors great trouble because they imply commitments other than the ones already made. If you use Durkheim to discuss Marxian ideas or the language of survey research to discuss an ethnographic study, you will probably find yourself working at cross purposes. Such confusions had caused the theoretical difficulties we discovered in our editing exercises in the seminar.

If you start writing early in your research—before you have all your data, for instance—you can begin cleaning up your thinking sooner. Writing a draft without data clarifies what you would like to discuss and, therefore, what data you will have to get. Writing can thus shape your research design. This differs from the more common notion that you do your research first and then "write it up." This extends the Flower-Hayes (1981) idea that the early phases of writing lead writers to see what they will have to do in the later stages.

Making your work clearer involves considerations of audience. Who is it supposed to be clearer for? Who will read what you write? What do they have to know so that they will not misread or find what you say obscure or unintelligible? You will write one way for the people you work with closely on a joint project, another way for professional colleagues in your subspecialty, still another for professional colleagues in other specialties and disciplines, and differently yet for an intelligent lay reader.

How can you find out what readers will understand? You can give your early drafts to sample members of your intended audience and ask them what they think. That's what the seminar members found so frightening and troublesome, because showing people early drafts could expose them to ridicule and shame. So the prescription, while simple, may not be workable. You can only show your less-than-perfect work to people if you have learned—as I hoped the seminar's members had from our class exercises—that you will not be harmed if people see it. Naturally, not everyone is a good audience for early drafts. We discovered that while editing each other's papers. Some people, finding it difficult to treat early drafts as early, insist on criticizing them with the standards appropriate to finished products. Some readers have better editorial judgment than others, and you need a circle of people you can trust to respond appropriately to the stage your work is in.

In addition to a theory of the act of writing, then, we also need a theory of the social organization of writing as a professional activity. Because most people write in absolute privacy, readers attribute the results to the author alone and credit or debit them to his or her professional reputational account. I use bookkeeping language because most people secretly think of it that way.

Why do writers work so privately? Most of them, as I said earlier, acquire their writing habits, complete with all the rituals designed to eliminate chaos and laughable results, in high school or college as adaptations to the situations they write in at that stage of their careers. The student's situation rewards quick, competent preparation of short, passable papers, not the skills of rewriting and redoing. (As Woody Allen once said, "Eighty percent of life is getting it done and handing it in on time.") Smart students—the smarter they are, the quicker they learn—don't bother with useless skills. The first draft, being the only one, counts.

Students find the skill of writing short papers quickly less useful as they advance in graduate school. During their first few years, they may, depending on the department, have to write the same kind of papers they wrote as undergraduates. But eventually they have to write longer papers, making more complex arguments based on more complicated data. Few people can write such papers in their heads and get it right on the first try, though students may naively think that good writers routinely do. ("Getting it right" means putting the argument so clearly that the paper begins by asserting what it later demonstrates.) So students flounder, fear "getting things wrong," and don't get it done on time. Writing at the last minute, they produce papers with interesting ideas, superficial coherence, and no clear underlying argument—interesting early drafts which they nevertheless want treated as end results.

Some young sociologists (and many other young scholars as well) get into situations after graduate work that reward that style of work even less. Scholarly disciplines do not furnish such neatly marked deadlines as schools do. There are no simple "on times." Of course, there are professional "on times": if you do not publish enough articles at a rate fast enough for your department or dean, you might not be promoted or get a raise or be able to find another job. But the timetables for these productions are loose and partly shaped by administrative whim, and people may mistakenly think that more pressing concerns—preparing lectures or other university work—require their immediate attention. Young scholars may thus find that time has slipped away and so they haven't met a production quota less explicit than that of the undergraduate years, one they let themselves ignore because the organization didn't press it on them.

When there's no conventionally fixed time at which a paper must be submitted and no single judge who will give it a grade, scholars work on their own schedules, at their own pace. They submit the results to that amorphous body of judges, "the professional community," or at least to the representatives of that community who edit journals, make up programs for professional meetings, and give editorial opinions to book publishers. Taken together, these readers embody the diversity of opinion and practice in the discipline. That diversity makes it likely that, in the long run, authors seldom go unpublished simply because they have the wrong views or work in the wrong style. So many organizations publish so many journals (and the number of new journals grows every day), and every point of view finds a home somewhere. But editors still reject papers or send them back with the dreaded instruction to "revise and resubmit" because they are mixed up—because their authors write unclearly or misstate the problem they want to address.

As a result, professional writing gets "privatized." No peer group shares the writer's problem. No group has the same paper to hand in on the same day. Everyone has a different paper to hand in whenever they get it ready. So sociological writers don't develop a culture, a body of shared solutions to their shared problems. As a result, a situation that has been called pluralistic ignorance arises. Everyone thinks that everyone else is getting it done and will be ready to hand it in on time. They keep their difficulties to themselves. This may be one reason sociologists and other scholars write in such isolation.

In any event, their work requires extensive rewriting and editorial work. Since the only version that counts is the last one, they have every reason to keep working on something until it is right. Not as right as it can be, given the time available—that's the college model—but as right as they can imagine it ever being.

This, naturally, is subject to some realistic constraints, so that it will get done sometime. Remember, though, that some major works have taken twenty years to prepare and that some scholars are willing to pay the price of slow production.

But many authors don't know how to rewrite and think that every version of anything they produce will be used to judge them. They are partly right. Such work will be used to make judgments, but if they are lucky, the judgments will be appropriate to the stage of work. So they don't produce, or they produce in very painful ways, attempting to get whatever they put on paper into perfect form before anyone sees it.

An interesting exception to this pattern occurs in group projects where, if the work is to proceed at all, the participants must occasionally produce documents bringing each other up to date. Participants in successful projects learn to look at each other's work as preliminary, thus relieving everyone of the necessity of producing perfect drafts the first time.

More commonly, writers solve the problem of isolation (as some always have) by developing a circle of friends who will read their work in the right spirit, treating as preliminary what is preliminary, helping the author sort out the mixed-up ideas of a very rough draft or smooth out the ambiguous language of a later version, suggesting references that might be helpful or comparisons that will give the key to some intractable puzzle. That circle may contain friends from your graduate school cohort, former professors, or people who share some interest with you. These relationships are usually reciprocal. As the trust between author and reader grows, the reader will ask the author to do some reading in return. Some promising relations of this kind die when the favor isn't returned.

Some people cannot read things in an appropriate way. They fixate on small things—sometimes just a word that could easily be replaced by one that avoids the problem—and can't think about or comment on anything else. Others, usually known far and wide as excellent editors, see the core problem and give helpful suggestions. Avoid the former. Search out the latter.

The above can be read as helpful hints suggested by the rudimentary theory of professional situations and writing problems I have been discussing. The seminar group, always interested in helpful hints, often lured me into pontificating about my experience. Although much of what I said in response to these seductions consisted of bad imitations of the kind old Mr. Chips, the hero of a now forgotten 1930s movie, a few of the concerns are worth mentioning.

Those who had some professional experience and had had papers rejected or sent back for extensive revision worried about how to respond to criticism. They frequently reverted to school talk: "Do I have to do such and such just because they said so?" They sometimes talked like artists whose masterwork had been mauled by philistines. I thought they were reverting to the attitude that sees most students through college, the notion that "they" are whimsical, have no real standards, and just decide things capriciously. If the authorities really don't have any stable standards you can't respond to their criticisms rationally, by inspecting the document you have created to see what it needs; instead you have to find out what they want and provide it. Authors found the evidence for this in the often contradictory advice they received from critics: one told them to take something out while another suggested they expand the same section.

My practical tip on this point was that readers are not clairvoyant, and therefore, when an author's prose is ambiguous or confused, they don't immediately see what was really meant, but produce their own, sometimes contradictory, interpretations. A common problem arose when an author began a paper by suggesting that it was going to deal with problem X and then proceeded to analyze, in a perfectly satisfactory way, problem Y, a characteristic fault of early drafts, easily cleaned up in revision. Some critics, spotting the confusion, will suggest that the analysis, or even the research, be redone so that the paper can really deal with X. Others, more realistic, tell the author to rewrite the introduction so that it says that the paper is about Y. But critics of both kinds are responding to the same confusion. The author need not do what any of them says, but should get rid of the confusion so that it will no longer be there to complain about.

Another problem the seminar members worried about was co-authorship, and the example came out of our own class. Toward the end of the term, when we had done everything I had planned and I was at a loss for entertainments to fill the remaining seminar hours, I suggested that we write a paper together on a topic we all knew something about: problems of writing in sociology. We took turns, in a variation of an old parlor game, dictating the next sentence of the paper. Each student added to the body of the text as it grew. Some tried to follow the line suggested by their predecessors. Some ignored it and began all over again. Some made cute remarks. Several wrote the sentences down as they were produced and read out the accumulation on request.

When we finished, we had eighteen sentences, and to everyone's surprise, despite all the non sequiturs and wisecracks, it wasn't a bad first draft, given the way we had agreed to appreciate and use first drafts. In fact, it was so interesting that I suggested we expand it for publication. That immediately raised a question: where should we publish it? We discussed the kinds of journals that might be interested in such a topic, and we finally decided on the *American Sociologist*, a journal devoted to professional problems which the American Sociological Association later, unfortunately, stopped publishing. I left the room to get some coffee. When I came back, the cozy atmosphere had degenerated. People were glowering at each other and confessed that they had, in my absence, begun quarreling over a predictable trouble. If some people did more work than others, who would put their names on the final paper and in what order?

This upset me. Many authors and contributors have fought over that very real question. I told them my solution: to give everyone credit who conceivably might have had anything to do with it. They quickly pointed out that a tenured full professor could afford such ideas, but students and younger scholars couldn't. I don't know if they were right or not, but the idea isn't foolish on its face.

We continued to talk and soon saw that only four or five students were really interested in pursuing the job. The seminar took place in the spring, and they agreed to work on it over the summer. Social organization intervened again. Graduate work is organized into classes that meet for a quarter or semester and then are over, and projects whose lives depend in some substantial way on money being available to sustain them. Since neither of these forms of automatic coordination existed beyond the end of the term during which the seminar occurred, the would-be coauthors had nothing to make them meet and continue their work, and they didn't. They never wrote the paper.

In some ways, this chapter is that paper, the residue of the work done by the participants in that class, and a lot of other people, by now too many to name, who offered suggestions on it (most of which I accepted) and participated in my classes over many years. When the organizations supporting collective work are that ephemeral, if the work is to be done at all (and usually it isn't), one of the survivors must take it on as an individual project. Which is what has happened here, if the collaboration I've described can be labeled an "individual" project.

2 : Persona and Authority

Rosanna Hertz, later a fully credentialed professional colleague but then a very advanced graduate student, came into my office one day and said she'd like to talk to me about a chapter of her thesis-in-progress, which I had edited for her. She said, in a careful tone which I intuited hid a certain amount of irritation, that she agreed that the writing was improved—shorter, clearer, on the whole much better. But, she said, she didn't quite understand the principles that governed what I had done. Could I go over the document with her and explain them? I told her that I wasn't sure what principles governed my editorial judgment, that I really edited by ear (I'll explain that expression, which does not mean that there are no rules at all, in chapter 4). But I agreed to do my best. I wondered whether I actually did follow any general principles of editing and thought that, if I did, I might discover what they were by trying to explain them to her.

Rosanna brought her chapter in a few days later. I had rewritten it extensively, cutting a lot of words but, I hoped, not losing any of her thought. It was a very good piece of work—rich data, imaginatively analyzed, well organized—but it was very wordy and academic. I had removed as much of the redundancy and academic flourish as I thought she would stand for. We went over it, a page at a time, and she quizzed me on each point. None of my changes involved technical sociological terms. Where she wrote "unified stance" I substituted "agreement," because it was shorter. I replaced "confronted the issue" with "talked about," because it was less pretentious. A longer example: where she wrote "This chapter will examine the impact of money or, more specifically, independent incomes on relations between husbands and wives with particular regard to the realm of financial affairs," I substituted "This chapter will show that independent incomes change the way husbands and wives handle financial affairs," for similar reasons. I removed meaningless qualifications ("tends to"), combined sentences that repeated long phrases, and when she said the same thing in two ways in successive sentences, took out the less effective version, explaining what I was doing and why as I went along.

She agreed with each of my ad hoc explanations, but we weren't discovering any general principles. I asked her to take over and work on a page of text I hadn't done anything to. We went over a few lines and then came to a sentence which said that the people she was studying "could afford not to have to be concerned with" certain things. I asked how she thought she could change that. She looked and looked at the sentence and finally said that she couldn't see any way to improve that phrasing. I finally asked if she could just say that they "needn't worry" about those things.

She thought about it, set her jaw, and decided that this was the place to make her stand. "Well, yes, that is shorter, and it certainly is clearer. . . ." The thought hung unfinished as blatantly as if she had spoken the ellipsis aloud. After a prolonged and momentous silence, I said, "But *what?*" "Well," she said, "the other way is *classier.*"

My intuition told me the word was important. I said that she could repay all the favors she owed me by writing five pages explaining exactly what she meant when she said "classier." She looked embarrassed—it's obvious now that I was taking unfair advantage both of friendship and professorial authority—and said she would. I couldn't blame her for making me wait a couple of months for those pages. She told me later that it was the hardest thing she had ever had to write because she knew she had to tell the truth.

I am going to quote from her letter at length. But this is not just a matter of one author's character and language. "Classier" was an important clue precisely because Rosanna was saying out loud what many students and professionals in the scholarly disciplines believed and felt but, less courageous, were less willing to admit. They'd hinted at what she finally wrote and the hints convinced me her attitude was widespread.

The letter I got was four double-spaced pages, and I won't quote all of it or quote it in sequence because Rosanna was thinking out loud when she wrote it and the order is not crucial. She began by remarking,

> Somewhere along the line, probably in college, I picked up on the fact that articulate people used big words, which impressed me. I remember taking two classes from a philosophy professor simply because I figured he must be really smart since I didn't know the meaning of the words he used in class. My notes from these classes are almost non-existent. I spent class time writing down the words he used that I didn't know, going home and looking them up. He sounded so smart to me simply because I didn't understand him. . . . The way someone writes—the more difficult the writing style—the more intellectual they sound.

It is no accident, as they say, that she learned to think this way in college. The excerpt expresses the perspective of a subordinate in a highly stratified organization. Colleges and universities, pretending to be communities of intellectuals who discuss matters of common interest freely and disinterestedly, are no such thing. Professors know more, have the degrees to prove it, test students and grade their papers, and in every imaginable way sit on top of the heap while students stand at the bottom. Some resent the inequality, but intelligent students who hope to be intellectuals themselves accept it wholeheartedly. They believe, like Rosanna, that the professors who teach them know more and should be imitated, whether what they do makes sense or not. The principle of hierarchy assures them that they are wrong and the teacher is right. They grant the same privileges to authors:

> When I read something and I don't know immediately what it means, I always give the author the benefit of the doubt. I assume this is a smart person and the problem with my not understanding the ideas is that I'm not as smart. I don't assume either that the emperor has no clothes or that the author is not clear because of their own confusion about what they have to say. I always assume that it is my inability to understand or that there is something more going on than I'm capable of understanding. . . . I assume if it got into the *AJS* [*American Journal of Sociology*], for example, chances are it's good and it's important and if I don't understand it that's my problem since the journal has already legitimated it.

She makes a further point, which other people mentioned as well. (Sociologists will recognize it as a specific instance of the general problem of socialization into professional worlds, as discussed, for example, in Becker and Carper 1956a and 1956b.) Graduate students learning to be academics know that they are not real intellectuals yet—just as medical students know they are not yet real doctors—and search eagerly for signs of progress. The arcane vocabulary and syntax of stereotypical academic prose clearly distinguish laypeople from professional intellectuals, just as the ability of professional ballet dancers to stand on their toes distinguishes them from ordinary folks. Learning to write like an academic moves students toward membership in that elite, as Rosanna's letter explained:

While I personally find scholarly writing boring and prefer to spend my time reading novels, academic elitism is a part of every graduate student's socialization. I mean that academic writing is not English but written in a shorthand that only members of the profession can decipher. . . . I think it is a way to . . . maintain group boundaries of elitism. . . . Ideas are supposed to be written in such a fashion that they are difficult for untrained people to understand. This is scholarly writing. And if you want to be a scholar you need to learn to reproduce this way of writing.

(This is as good a place as any to note that, in writing the excerpts I have been quoting, Rosanna deliberately adopted a point of view she has since abandoned. When I asked her, she said that she no longer thinks that writing style has anything to do with intelligence or the complexity of ideas.)

She gave some examples of "classy" writing she had caught herself at, with explanations of why she found these locutions attractive:

Instead of choosing to write "he lives at," I prefer "he resides at." Instead of saying "Couples spend their extra money" (or "additional money" or even "disposable income") I'd choose "surplus income." It sounds more grown-up. Here's a favorite of mine: "predicated upon the availability of" is classier than saying "exists because of" [or, for that matter, "depends on"]. Maybe it sounds more awesome. Here's another one. I could say "domestic help" but what I choose to do is say "third party labor." The first time I use it I put a "that is" after the phrase and explain it. Then I am at liberty to use "third party labor" throughout, and it sounds fancier. I think the point here is that I am looking for a writing style that makes me sound smart.

None of these classy locutions mean anything different from the simpler ones they replace. They work ceremonially, not semantically.

Writing in a classy way to sound smart means writing to sound like, maybe even be, a certain kind of person. Sociologists, and other scholars, do that because they think (or hope) that being the right kind of person will persuade others to accept what they say as a persuasive social science argument. C. Wright Mills said that the

> lack of ready intelligibility [in scholarly writing], I believe, usually has little or nothing to do with the complexity of the subject matter, and nothing at all with profundity of thought. It has to do almost entirely with certain confusions of the academic writer about his own status. . . . In large part sociological habits of style stem from the time when sociologists had little status even with other academic men. Desire for status is one reason why academic men slip so easily into unintelligibility. . . . To overcome the academic prose you have first to overcome the academic pose. (Mills 1959, 218–19, emphasis in the original.)

Living as an intellectual or academic makes people want to appear smart, in the sense of clever or intelligent, to themselves and others. But not only smart. They also want to appear knowledgeable or worldly or sophisticated or down-home or professional—all sorts of things, many of which they can hint at in the details of their writing. They hope that being taken for such a person will make what they say believable. We can explore what people mean when they talk or think about writing in a "classy" way, or in any other way, through the idea of a *persona*, if I can be forgiven that classy term. Although writers display their personae through the devices of style, I will not discuss style at length. Strunk and White (1959) and Williams (1981) are still first among many who analyze style and show writers how to use its elements effectively, and readers should pursue the subject there. I want to emphasize how writers use personae to try get readers to accept their arguments.

Just as a Briton's accent tells listeners the speaker's class, a scholar's prose tells readers what kind of person is doing the writing. Many sociologists and other scholars, both students and professionals, want to be "classy" people, the kind of people who talk and write *that* way. Writing classy prose, they try to be (or at least create the appearance of being) classy.

But what is a classy person, to a young or even middle-aged scholar? My guesses about the content of these fantasies may be wrong and dated (since conceptions of such qualities change all the time). In fact, fantasies of classiness vary so much that no one characterization will do justice to all of them. At the time, I imagined it this way: a classy person, to a young professorial type (male, in that era) wears a tweed jacket with leather patches at the elbow, smokes a pipe (the men, anyway), and sits around the senior common room swilling port and discussing the latest issue of the *Times Literary Supplement* or the *New York Review of Books* with a bunch of similar people. Mind you, I don't mean that the people who have these fantasies really want to be like that. The stylish young woman whose remark provoked this meditation wouldn't have been caught dead in such an outfit. But they want to talk like such a person. Perhaps not *that* person exactly, but the image gives the general flavor.

Whether or not some young academics and academics-in-training want to be classy, the possibility reminds us that everyone writes as someone, affects a character, adopts a persona who does the talking for them. Literary analysts know that, but seldom examine its implications for academic writing. Academics favor a few classic personae whose traits color academic prose, shape academic arguments, and make the resulting writing more or less persuasive to various audiences. Those personae inhabit a world of scholars, researchers, and intellectuals in which it is useful or comfortable to be one or another of these people.

The academic-intellectual world has an ambiguous and uneasy relation to the ordinary world, and many academics worry about their own relation to ordinary people. Do we really differ from them enough to warrant the privileged lives we feel entitled to and sometimes actually lead? When we claim to be thinking hard about something, though we are visibly just loafing in a chair, should other people let us do that? Why should we have months off from regular work "just to think?" And, especially, should anyone pay any attention to *what* we think? Why? The persona we adopt when we write tells readers (and by extension all the potential skeptics) who we are and why we should be believed, and that answers all the other questions.

Some personae authors adopt—general human types— directly address the problem of the relations between intellectuals and laypeople. Many personae emphasize the differences between *us* and *them*—our superiority in important areas—that justify our lives and show why everyone should believe us. When we present ourselves as classy, we want to see ourselves and have others see us as worldly, sophisticated, "smart" in both common-sense meanings. (Becoming an intellectual has helped enough people move up in the class system that it would be silly to ignore that meaning of "classy.") If we write in a classy way, then, we show that we are generally smarter than ordinary people, have finer sensibilities, understand things they don't, and thus should be believed.

This persona is the one that leads us to use fancy language, substitute big words for little ones, esoteric terms for commonplace ones, and elaborate sentences making subtle distinctions that Rosanna had found so compelling. Our language strives for the elegance we would like to embody and feel.

Other writers adopt personae that emphasize their esoteric expertise. They like to appear knowledgeable, to be the kind of person who knows "inside stuff" ordinary folks will have to wait to read about in next week's newspaper. Most specialists in matters that concern laypeople in some way—labor relations, domestic politics, or perhaps some country which gets itself into the news—love to let people in on what only they know. "Inside dopesters," as David Riesman once called them, let readers know who they are by a wealth of detail, mostly unexplained. They write as though their audience consisted of people who knew almost as much about it, or at least about its background— whatever *it* is—as they do. They mention dates, names, and places only a specialist will recognize, and don't explain. The barrage of detailed knowledge overwhelms readers, who feel compelled to accept the author's argument. How could someone who knows all that be wrong? (I have foregone including detailed examples both because they are so easily available and because each field has its own variations, which I hope readers will find and analyze for themselves.)

James Clifford has described the classic anthropological persona, invented (more or less) by Bronislaw Malinowski, which persuades the reader that the argument being made is correct because, after all, the anthropologist *was there*: "Malinowski gives us the imago of the new 'anthropologist'—squatting by the campfire, looking, listening and questioning, recording and interpreting Trobriand life. The literary charter of this new authority is the first chapter of *Argonauts* [*of the Western Pacific*], with its prominently displayed photographs of the ethnographer's tent pitched among the Kiriwinian dwellings" (Clifford 1983, 123).

Clifford identifies some of the stylistic devices Malinowski used to project the I-was-there persona: sixty-six photographs, a "Chronological List of Kula Events Witnessed by the Writer," and a "constant alternation between impersonal description of typical behavior and statements on the order of 'I witnessed . . .' and 'Our party, sailing from the North. . . .'" He calls these devices claims to "experiential authority":

> based on a "feel" for the foreign context, a kind of
> accumulated savvy and sense of the style of a people or
> place. . . . Margaret Mead's claim to grasp the underlying
> principle or ethos of a culture through a heightened
> sensitivity to form, tone, gesture, and behavioral styles,
> or Malinowski's stress on his life in the village and the
> comprehension derived from the "imponderibilia" of daily
> existence are cases in point (Clifford 1983, 128).

Sociologists who do fieldwork in the anthropological style use similar devices to display a persona whose claim to authority rests on intimate knowledge. William Foote Whyte's description (1943, 14–25) of bowling with the out-of-work men he studied, known to every sociologist, is a classic example.

I gave samples of classy writing from Rosanna Hertz. It is much harder to give examples of writing that projects an authoritative persona. Writing only has that character in relation to an audience. Naming the first president of the Bagel Makers' Union and giving the date of the passage of the Wagner Act will not affect a nonspecialized reader as it does a labor relations expert. So authoritativeness is not inherent in any piece of writing. These devices only work on an audience unfamiliar with the area. (But it might be necessary to use the same devices to convince experts that you know what you are talking about. An expert in photographic history once warned me that a paper I had written about photography would be ignored by her colleagues because I had incorrectly spelled Mathew Brady's name with two *ts* and Georgia O'Keeffe's with one *f*.)

Many academic personae make authors appear generally authoritative, entitled to the last word on whatever they are talking about. Authors who adopt these personae love to correct lay errors, to tell readers definitively what will happen in some delicate international situation whose outcome we can't imagine, to explain what "we scientists" or "we sociologists" know about things laypeople have the wrong idea about.

These authorities speak in imperatives: "We must recognize . . ." "We cannot ignore . . ." They speak impersonally, talk about "one" doing things rather than using the first person. (Some grammarians think that "one" substitutes for the second person and cannot be used in place of the first person. They must never have met authorities like the ones I know and read.) These authorities use the passive voice to convey how little what they say depends on them personally, how much, rather, it reflects the reality their unique knowledge gives them access to. Latour and Woolgar (1979) were among the first to show that laboratory scientists habitually use a typical authoritative style which conceals any traces of the ordinary human activity that produced their results.

Some writers—I favor this persona myself—take a Will Rogers line. We are just plain folks who emphasize our similarity to ordinary people, rather than the differences. We may know a few things others don't, but it's nothing special. "Shucks, you'd of thought the same as me if you'd just been there to see what I seen. It's just that I had the time or took the trouble to be there, and you didn't or couldn't, but let me tell you about it." Something like that. (In fact, this whole book is an extended example of that persona.)

Such writers want to use their similarity to others, their ordinariness, to persuade readers that what they are saying is right. We write more informally, favor the personal pronoun, and appeal to what we-and-the-reader know in common rather than what we know and the reader doesn't. Every style, then, is the voice of someone the author wants to be, or be taken for.

This analysis of personae may suggest that there is something illegitimate about speaking in any of these ways. Clearly, you can use these devices illegitimately, to disguise inadequacies of evidence or argument. But we will often, quite reasonably if not logically, accept an argument in part just because the author clearly knows the field (including presidents of the Bagel Makers' Union) or has a general cultural sophistication we respect. Since the author can't be nobody, every author will necessarily be somebody. It might as well be someone readers respect and believe.

The list of available personae varies among academic disciplines, because one source of personae is famous teachers or characters in a field. Admiring their teachers, students imitate not only their personal mannerisms, but also the way they write, especially when that style projects a distinctive personality. Thus, many philosophers adopted the diffident, tentative, arrogant persona and the worrying, conversational prose style of Ludwig Wittgenstein, just as many sociologists who take up ethnomethodology decorate their papers with the endless lists and qualifications of its founder, Harold Garfinkel.

Imitating teachers is the specific form of a general tendency to indicate theoretical and political allegiances by the way you write. Scholars worry a lot about which "school" they belong to, with good reason. Many highly factionalized fields reward and punish people on ghe basis of the allegiances they display. Disciplines seldom do that as rigorously or ruthlessly as authors think, but nervous scholars don't just imagine the dangers. You can easily demonstrate your allegiances by using a school's code words, which differ from the words adherents of other schools use, in part, because the theories they belong to in fact give them a slightly different meaning. Most sociological theories rely, for instance, on the idea that people remake society continuously by doing, day in and day out, the things that reaffirm that that is the way things are done. You might say that people create society by acting as though it existed. You might say, if you were a Marxist theorist, that people reproduce social relations through daily practice. If you were a symbolic interactionist, or an adherent of Berger and Luckmann, you might speak of the social construction of reality.

These are not just different words. They express different thoughts. Still, not that different. Code words don't always contain a core of unique meaning, but we still use them rather than some other words that might lead people to think that we belong, or would like to belong, to some other school of thought. The allegiance-signaling purpose of stylistic devices is clearest when the author says things that conflict with the theory the language signals, when the desire to say "I am a functionalist" or "I am a Marxist" overcomes the desire to say what you mean. (Stinchcombe [1982] elaborates this idea in an article cited and discussed in chapter 8.)

John Walton, reading an earlier version of this material and thinking over his experience teaching a seminar something like mine, points out that often

people want very much to show their theoretical colors, to signal to the hip reader (professor or editor) that they are on the right side of a controversial issue. I see that most with writing that wants to communicate sophistication in Marxism without appearing as "orthodox" or susceptible to being branded as such. A term like "social formation" dropped in the right place says what you want to other sophisticates, without carrying much risk.

Walton puts an important point into that parenthesis—that we want to signal somebody in particular, not an abstraction. Who we want to signal depends on the arena we are operating in, and arenas are often more local than scholarly writers realize, particularly for students. The sociologists and other professors I saw in the 1960s and 1970s in Chicago had different worries and made different criticisms than those Walton saw in Davis, California, and we both had larger professional audiences which differed as well.

Remember that academic writers take on many allegiances to schools and political positions while still in graduate school. That accounts for another major source of stylistic problems. When I argued with students about how they wrote—as when I suggested to Rosanna Hertz that she write in a way she thought less classy—they told me that I was wrong because that *was* the way sociologists wrote. I spent a lot of time arguing about that before I saw their point.

The point is professionalization. Academics-in-training worry about whether they are yet, can ever be, or even want to be professional academics of the kind they are changing themselves into. Second- or third- or fourth-year graduate students have not taken binding vows. They may have second thoughts. Nor have they been finally chosen. They might flunk out. Their committee might turn their theses down. Who knows what might happen?

That uncertainty creates yet another reason for magical thinking and practice. If you act as though you already were a sociologist, you might fool everyone into accepting you as one, and even take it seriously yourself. Writing is one of the few ways a graduate student can act like a professional. Just as medical students can only do a few of things real doctors routinely do, graduate students do not become professionals until they get their PhD degrees. Until then, they can teach as graduate assistants and work on other people's projects, but ordinarily will not be taken as seriously as people with degrees. At least, they think that's true, and (depending on the time and place) they may be mostly right. So they adopt what they see around them, the style professional journal articles and books they read are written in, as an appropriate signal of their guild membership.

What kind of writing will do that for them? Not writing plain English prose. Anyone can do that, they think. Students share the attitudes of many art audiences toward "ordinary" modes of expression:

> Artistic innovators frequently try to avoid what they regard as the excessive formalism, sterility, and hermeticism of their medium by exploiting the actions and objects of everyday life. Choreographers like Paul Taylor and Brenda Way use running, jumping, and falling down as conventionalized dance movements, instead of the more formal movements of classical ballet, or even of traditional modern dance. . . . [But] less involved audiences look precisely for the conventional formal elements the innovators replace to distinguish art from nonart. They do not go to the ballet to see people run, jump, and fall down; they can see that anywhere. They go instead to see people do the difficult and esoteric formal movements that signify "real dancing." The ability to see ordinary material as art material—to see that the running, jumping, and falling down are not just that, but are the elements of a different language of the medium— thus distinguishes serious audience members from the well-socialized member of the culture, the irony being that these materials are perfectly well known to the latter, although not as art materials (Becker 1982a, 49–50).

Students act like that too. They know plain English but don't want to express their hard-earned knowledge in it. Remember the student who said, "Gee, Howie, if you say it that way it sounds like something anyone could say." If you want to convince yourself that the time and effort spent getting your degree are worth it, that you are changing" in some way that will change your life, then you want to look different from everyone else, not the same. That accounts for a truly crazy cycle in which students repeat the worst stylistic excesses the journals contain, learn that those very excesses are what makes their work different from what every damn fool knows and says, write more articles like those they learned from, and submit them to journals whose editors publish them.

Why do editors do that? Because nothing better is available. Because the number of journals has increased astronomically and the number of knowledgeable people available to do the required peer review is not large enough to handle the load which Andrew Abbott, for many years editor of the *American Journal of Sociology*, tells us leads to this work being done not by the knowledgeable senior scholar the term "peer review" implies but rather by graduate students who jump at the chance to do this grown-up job (Abbott 1999, 190–91). And so the journals provide the raw material for another generation to learn bad habits from.

These conditions are historically specific and change as the social organizations people work in change. The conditions of publication (organizationally based as they are) change, the work situations of editors and readers change, and what's expected, even required, of authors changes. And that changes common knowledge—we might call it "public opinion" among members of the trade—the things people learn from experience they can say, believe, and act on without being punished for it. I take those changes up in chapter 10.

3 : One Right Way

Scholarly writers have to organize their material and say what they say clearly enough for readers to follow the reasoning and accept the conclusions. They make this job harder than it needs to be when they think there is only One Right Way to do it, that each paper they write has a preordained structure they must find. They simplify their work, on the other hand, when they recognize that there are many effective ways to say something and that their job is only to choose one and execute it so that readers know what they are doing.

I have a lot of trouble with students (and not just students) when I go over their papers and suggest revisions. They get tongue-tied and act ashamed and upset when I say that this is a good start, all you have to do is this, that, and the other and it will be in good shape. Why are they so leery of rewriting?

In the precomputer era, when "cut" and "paste" were laborious physical work instead of keyboard commands, laziness might have explained this reluctance. We move our prose around more easily now. But students and scholars still balk at rewriting, though the cost is more a psychological one these days. Students are still subordinates in a hierarchical organization: a school. The master-servant or boss-worker relationship characteristic of schools gives people a lot of reasons for not wanting to rewrite, many of them quite sensible. Teachers and administrators intend their schools' systems of reward to encourage learning. But those systems usually teach undergraduates, instead, to earn grades rather than to be interested in the subjects they study or to do a great job. (This discussion is based on the research reported in Becker, Geer, and Hughes 1968. I don't know any later research that addresses these specific points, but people act and talk as though nothing has changed that much since our long-ago study.) Students try to find out, by interrogating instructors and relying on the experience of other students, exactly what they have to do to get good grades. When they find out, they do what they have learned is necessary, and no more. Few students learn (and here we can all rely on our own memories as students and teachers) that they have to rewrite or revise anything. On the contrary, they learn that a smart student does a paper once, making it as good as possible in one pass. If you really don't care very much about the work you are doing—if it is just a chore to be done for a course, and you have calculated that it is worth only so much effort and no more—then you might reasonably do it once and the hell with it. You have better ways to spend your time.

Schools also teach students to think of writing as a kind of test: the teacher hands you the problem, and you try to answer it, then go on to the next problem. One shot per problem. Going over it is, somehow, "cheating," especially when you have had the benefit of someone else's coaching after your first try. It's somehow no longer a fair test of your own abilities. You can hear your sixth grade teacher saying, "Is this all your own work?" What a student might think of as coaching and cheating, of course, is what more experienced people think of as getting some critical response from informed readers.

Joseph Williams suggested to me, many years ago, that students, being young, simply don't have the experience of life that would let them use their imaginations to get out of their own egocentric worlds. So they thus can't imagine either an audience's response to the text they have already produced or the possibility of a text other than that one. But the lack of experience may result less from youth than from the way schools infantilize young people. Graduate students certainly appreciate the need for rewriting more keenly when, later in a student's career, they contemplate reading their paper at a professional meeting; they envision for the first time total strangers assaulting their logic, evidence, and prose.

Such reasons might explain why people don't rewrite, but not the shame and embarrassment they feel at the thought of doing it. These feelings also originate in schools. No one connected with schools, neither teachers nor administrators, tells students how the writing they read—textbooks or their own teachers' publications, for instance—actually gets done. The separation of scholarly work from teaching in almost all colleges and universities hides the process from students. (Just as, according to Thomas Kuhn, histories of science hide all the false turns and mistakes in the research programs that produced the successes they celebrate.) Students don't know, never having seen their teachers (let alone textbook authors) at work, that all these people do things more than once, rather than treating their professional work as a quasi-test. Students don't know that journal editors routinely send papers back for revision, that publishers hire editors to improve the prose of books to be published. They don't know that revising and editing happen to everyone, and are not emergency procedures undertaken only in cases of scandalously unprofessional incompetence.

Students think of their teachers, and the authors of the texts their teachers give them as assignments to read, as authorities for another obvious reason: these people stand above them in the school hierarchy. They are the bosses who give the grades and judge whether students' work is good enough. Unless students decide that the educational institutions they attend are frauds (and surprisingly few do, considering the evidence available to them), they will accept the implicit organizational proposition that the people who run the schools they attend know what they are doing. Not only, then, do their academic superiors—as far as they can see—never rewrite anything, they also get what they write "right" the first time. So students learn and really believe, at least for a while, that "real writers" (or "professionals" or "smart people") get it right the first time. Only dummies have to do it over and over. This might be another version of the test mentality: the belief that being able to do it right the first time shows superior ability. This, too, is hierarchy, full-blown, at its worst: subordinates taking such evaluations as grades and teachers' comments, which are legitimated by the stratification of schools and scholarship, as ultimate and not-to-be-questioned evaluations of their own personal worth. (Becker, Geer, and Hughes 1968, 116–28, detail the evidence for this interpretation. To my knowledge, no one has disputed this characterization.)

All these ideas—about not rewriting, about the school paper as a sign of worth—rest on the fallacious premise that there is a "right answer," a "best way" to do things. Some readers will think I have invented a straw man, that serious students and scholars know there is no One Right Way. But students and scholars do believe in One Right Way, because the institutions they work in embody that idea. The ideas of "the right answer" and "a best way" find their natural home in hierarchy. Most people believe that the higher-ups in hierarchical organizations know more and know better than the people lower down. They don't. Studies of organizations show that superiors may know more about some things, but usually know a good deal less about many others. They even know less about the organization's central business, which you might suppose they would know better. But the official theory of the organization, and usually of its environing society, ignores such results, holding that higher-ups really *do* know better. What they know is, in fact, by definition, the "right answer."

No matter that real authorities know that there is never one right answer on any given subject, just a lot of provisional answers competing for attention and acceptance. Students, undergraduates particularly, don't like such talk. Why bother learning something that isn't true only to have to learn something else in its place tomorrow? Nor do true-believing scholars like it, whether they have discovered the truth themselves, or are only followers of the discoverers. The leaders of the field must know. What they know is what's in the book. That is real hierarchy, seen most clearly when a chemistry experiment performed in class fails to produce the "correct" result and the teacher tells students what should have happened and what, therefore, they should write in their notebooks. (Yes, that *does* happen.)

If there is one right answer, and you believe that the guardians who run the institution you work in know it, then you know that your job is to find out the right answer and reproduce it when required, thus showing that you deserve to be rewarded, maybe even to become one of the guardians yourself. That is the undergraduate version. A slightly more sophisticated version afflicts graduate students and professionals. Since what you are writing is something new, the One Right Way does not exist, but its Platonic ideal exists somewhere and it is up to you to discover it and put it down on paper. I suppose that many of us would like readers to feel that we have found such a preordained right way to say what we say, one that looks as though it could only be that way. But serious writers discover that perfect form (that is, some form that does what they want done, even though not the only possible one) after lengthy exploration, not the first time.

Sociologist Harvey Molotch put the point like this in a note to me:

A problem that writing people have is the idea in their heads that a given sentence, paragraph or paper must be the right one. Their training in a land of "facts," in the celebration of "right answers"—including the "right" way to approach their Chem lab book or English theme—immobilizes them at the keyboard. Their problem is that there are many right sentences, many right structures for an essay. . . . We have to free ourselves from the idea that there is only one CORRECT way. When we don't, the contradiction with reality absolutely stifles us since no sentence, paragraph or paper is demonstrable (to ourselves) as clearly the right one. Students watch their words come out, but of course these words—in first draft—are not even meeting the test of "OK," much less CORRECT and PERFECT ESSENCE OF CORRECT. Not having a vision of tentativeness, of first-draft, of n-draft, they can only feel frustration at the sight of failure. After a while, one sees the first tentative *thoughts* of a paragraph or paper as obviously failing this test—and so one doesn't even start: writer's cramp. The fear of failure is an *accurate* fear, because *nobody* could pass this self-imposed test of getting the one correct version, and the failure to do so is especially (and distressingly) evident at the point of first-draft.

Some very common, quite specific writing difficulties have their origins in this attitude: the problem of getting started and the problem of "which way to organize it." Neither one has a unique solution to be discovered. Whatever you do will be a compromise between conflicting possibilities. That doesn't mean that you can't arrive at workable solutions, only that you can't count on finding the one perfect solution that was there all along waiting for you to find it.

Most writers, even professionals, have trouble getting started. They start over and over again, working the first sentence or paragraph again and again as they find each successive attempt unsatisfactory in some new way. They start that way because they believe that there is One Right Way. If they can only find the Right Way to begin, they think, everything else will take care of itself, all the other problems that they fear are lurking ahead of them will disappear. With this unrealistic idea in their heads, they set themselves up to fail.

Suppose I am reporting on my study of Chicago schoolteachers.

(I have immodestly used this ancient document, my own PhD thesis, as an example because I know it well, and because the problems it exemplifies still bother students, who find the solutions I discuss helpful.) The study dealt with, loosely speaking, race, class, professional culture, and institutional organization. How shall I begin? I could say: "Schoolteacher culture defines lower-class, and especially black, students as difficult to work with. As a result, teachers avoid working in those schools, transferring to higher-class schools as soon as their seniority makes it possible, and that in turn means that lower-class schools are always staffed by new, inexperienced teachers." Even though I am talking about a thesis completed and accepted in 1951, I still have trouble writing a concise introductory sentence. (Imagine me trying to do it in 1951, when I still wasn't sure what the thesis was about.) When I look at the sentence I just typed, I might think, "Wait a minute, do I *really* want to say 'schoolteacher culture'? After all, it's not exactly culture in the strict anthropological sense, is it? I mean, they don't pass it on from generation to generation, and it doesn't cover all aspects of life; it isn't really a 'design for living.' If I call it culture, I'm sure to get in trouble, and I'll deserve it, because I will be saying something I might not mean." So I put that imaginary sheet in the imaginary wastebasket, and try again.

I might substitute "shared beliefs" for "culture" and feel happier with that. But then I would see that I was talking about class and remember what a tangle of implications surrounds every one of the many ways sociologists talk about class. Whose version would I mean? W. Lloyd Warner's? Karl Marx's? I might decide to go back over the literature on class again before using such an expression. So I would start over again. But now I might notice that I had said, "As a result of something teachers something-or-other." That is a pretty direct causal statement. Do I really think that social causality works like that? Shouldn't I use some less committing expression? In short, every way to say it would start me down some path I hadn't fully explored and might not want to take if I really understood what it would commit me to.

The simplest remarks have implications I might not like, and I wouldn't even know I was implying them. (Curious readers can see what I actually did by consulting Becker 1980.)

That is why people make outlines. Maybe working the whole puzzle out in outline will show you where you are going, help you catch all the implications, evade all the traps, and get it all to come out right. You will find the One Right Way. An outline can help you get started, even if it won't find the Way, but only if it is so detailed as to be the actual paper whose skeleton it pretends to be. That just gives you the same problem in a slightly different form.

Introductions raise the problem of unwanted implications in a specially difficult way. Everett Hughes told me, when I was still in graduate school, to write introductions last. "Introductions are supposed to introduce. How can you introduce something you haven't written yet? You don't know what it is. Get it written and then you can introduce it." If I do that, I discover that I have a variety of possible introductions available, each one *right* in some way, each giving a slightly different twist to my thought. I don't have to find the One Right Way to say what I want to say; I have to find out what I want to say. But I can do that more easily after I have said it all and know pretty much what I mean than when I am writing the first sentence. If I write my introductory sentences after I finish the body of my text, the problem of the One Right Way is less compelling.

Fearing commitment to the implications of an initial formulation also accounts for people beginning with the vacuous sentences and paragraphs so common in scholarly writing. "This study deals with the problem of careers"; or "Race, class, professional culture, and institutional organization all affect the problem of public education." Those sentences employ a typical evasive maneuver, pointing to something without saying anything, or anything much, about it. *What* about careers? How do all those things affect public education? People who make outlines do the same thing by making topic rather than sentence outlines.

The minute you turn the topic headings into non-vacuous sentences, the problems the outline solved return.

Many social scientists, however, think they are actually doing a good thing by beginning evasively. They reveal items of evidence one at a time, like clues in a detective story, expecting readers to keep everything straight until they triumphantly produce the dramatic concluding paragraph that summarizes argument and evidence at once. They may do this out of a scientific prudery which forbids stating a conclusion before laying out all the evidence (which ignores the excellent example of mathematical proofs that begin by stating the proposition to be proved). Investigators frequently report survey research results this way. A table shows, for example, that class and racial prejudice are directly related. The next table shows that that is true only when you hold education constant. Further tables showing the effect of age or ethnicity complicate matters further, and so on down a long road of items before whatever conclusion the assemblage warrants finally appears.

I often suggest to these would-be Conan Doyles that they simply put their last triumphant paragraph first, telling readers where the argument is going and what all this material will finally demonstrate. That flushes out the other reason for this caginess: "If I give the ending away at the beginning, no one will read the rest of what I've written." But scientific papers seldom deal with material suspenseful enough to warrant the format. If you put the paragraph that gives the secret away at the beginning, you can then go back and say explicitly what each section of your work contributes to reaching that result, instead of having to hide its function in noncommittal prose.

Suppose you are reporting, as Prudence Rains (1971) did, the results of a study of single mothers (then commonly referred to as "unwed mothers"). You *could*, in classical evasive style, begin your book like this: "This study investigates the experiences of single mothers, with special attention to their careers, moral aspects of their situations, and the influence of social agencies."

Giving nothing at all away, that beginning would leave the reader with a collection of unrelated tokens to be exchanged later in the book (if the author delivers on the I.O.U., never a sure thing) for sentences asserting real relationships between real entities.

Fortunately, Rains didn't do that. She wrote, instead, a model introduction, which explains exactly what the rest of the book then analyzes in detail. I quote it at length:

> Becoming an unwed mother is the outcome of a particular sequence of events that begins with forays into intimacy and sexuality, results in pregnancy, and terminates in the birth of an illegitimate child. Many girls do not have sexual relations before marriage. Many who do, do not get pregnant. And most girls who get pregnant while unmarried do not end up as unwed mothers. Girls who become unwed mothers, in this sense, share a common career that consists of the steps by which they came to be unwed mothers rather than brides, the clients of abortionists, contraceptively prepared lovers, or virtuous young ladies.
>
> The most significant aspects of this career are moral ones, for sexuality, pregnancy, and motherhood are matters closely linked to conceptions of feminine respectability and [are] intimately connected to women's conceptions of themselves. Becoming an unwed mother is not simply a private and practical trouble; it is the kind of trouble that forces public accounting, raises retrospective questions, and, above all, calls into question the kind of person the unwed mother was and is.
>
> The moral career of an unwed mother is, in this sense, like the moral careers of other persons whose acts are treated as deviant, and whose selves become publicly implicated. Important, if not central, to the moral career of such a person are the social agencies with which he may come into contact as a result of his situation. Social agencies and institutions, whether geared to rehabilitation, incarceration,

help, or punishment, provide and enforce interpretations of the person's current situation, of the past that led to it, and of the possibilities that lie ahead (Rains 1971, 1–2.).

That introduction, laying out the map of the trip the author is going to take them on, lets readers connect any part of the argument with its overall structure. Readers with such a map seldom get confused or lost.

Evasive vacuous sentences, however, are actually good ways to begin early drafts. They give you some leeway at a time when you don't want or need to be committed, and most important, they let you start. Write one down and you can go ahead without worrying that you have put your foot on a wrong path, because you haven't really taken a step yet. You just have to remember, when you have written the rest of what you have to say, to go back and replace these placeholders with real sentences that say what you mean.

Suppose I take this advice and start somewhere else. If I don't begin at the beginning, where do I begin? What do I write first? Won't anything I write commit me as much as a first sentence? Doesn't every sentence somehow contain in itself, at least by implication, the whole argument? Sure. So what? Remember that any sentence can be changed, rewritten, thrown out, or contradicted. That lets you write anything at all. No sentence commits, not because it doesn't prefigure your argument in just the way people fear, but because nothing bad will happen if it is wrong. You can write utter nonsense, things that turn out not to be what you think at all, and nothing will happen. Try it.

Once you know that writing a sentence down won't hurt you, know it because you have tried it, you can do what I usually ask people to try: write whatever comes into your head, as fast as you can, without reference to outlines, notes, data, books, or any other aids. The object is to find out what you would like to say, what all your earlier work on the topic or project has already led you to believe. This is the device known to teachers of composition as "freewriting," which I first heard of in Elbow (1981, 13–19) and then found in a less academic form in Anne Lamott's *Bird by Bird* (1994, 21–27), where it got the less academic name of "shitty first draft."

If you can bring yourself to do this (Pamela Richards discusses the reasons people shy away from doing it in chapter 6), you will make some interesting discoveries. If you follow the directions and write whatever comes into your head, you will find that you do not have the bewildering variety of choices you feared. You can see, once you have your work on paper, that most of it consists of slight variations on a very few themes. You do know what you want to say and, once you have the different versions before you, you can easily see how trivial the differences are. Or if there are real differences (though there seldom are), you now know what your choices are.

(The same trick helps students who get hung up trying to frame a dissertation topic. Ask them to write down, in no more than one or two sentences, one hundred different thesis ideas. Few people get past twenty or twenty-five before they see that they only have two or three ideas, which are almost always variations on a common theme.)

If you write this way, you usually find out, by the time you get to the end of your draft, what you have in mind. Your last paragraph reveals to you what the introduction ought to contain, and you can go back and put it in and then make the minor changes in other paragraphs your newfound focus requires.

In short, by the time we come to write something, we have done a lot of thinking. We have an investment in everything we have already worked out that commits us to a point of view and a way of handling the problem. We probably couldn't, even if we wanted to, handle the problem any differently from the way we will end up handling it. We are committed, not by the choice of a word, but by the analysis we have already done, by all our prior thinking and actions. That's why it makes no difference how we begin. We chose our path and destination a long time ago.

Writing an unthought-out, unplanned draft (what Joy Charlton once inelegantly but accurately called a "spew" draft, anticipating Lamott's terminology) demonstrates something else. You can't deal with the welter of thoughts that flash through your head when you stare at your screen trying to think where to begin. No one can. The fear of that chaos is one reason for the rituals the students in my seminar described. First one thing, then another, comes into your head. By the time you have thought the fourth thought, the first one is gone. For all you know, the fifth thought is the same as the first. In a short time, certainly, you have gone through your whole repertoire. How many thoughts can we have on one topic?

That's why it's so important to write a draft rather than to keep on preparing and thinking about what you will write when you do start. You have to give the thoughts a physical embodiment, *to write them down in some permanent form.* A thought written down (and not immediately thrown into the trash) is stubborn, doesn't change its shape, can be compared with the other thoughts that come after it. You can only learn how few thoughts you really have if you write them all down, set them side by side and compare them. That's one reason why dictating an early draft into your mobile device or computer is useful. The recording's invisible physical form makes the thought somehow less committing. It seems to make the words "real," but at the same time less likely to commit you to "dangerous" positions. Just the opposite. It makes writing the first sentences easier by letting you find out what you want to say.

A problem as insoluble as how to begin—another version of it, in fact—is how to organize what you have to say. Students often complain that they can't decide how to organize their material, whether to say this or that first, whether to use this idea as an organizing principle or that one. The theory of One Right Way to do things causes mischief here too. Another example from my thesis will provide material for the analysis.

I had simple results to report. Schoolteachers evaluated a number of aspects of their job: their relationships with the students they taught, the students' parents, the principal they worked for, and the other teachers they worked with. They liked those people in each category who made their work easier, disliked those who made it harder. In their view, schools varied most importantly in the social class of their students. They categorized children and parents by their own version of a social class system. They described "slum children" (their term, which covered most but not all African American children and a sizeable portion of white children as well) difficult to teach. They found upper-middle class students difficult too, smart but not respectful enough of the teacher's age and authority. Most teachers preferred working-class children, who could do ordinary schoolwork but were docile and thus easy to handle. They also preferred working-class parents, who were most helpful in controlling their own children. The then common (and by no means gone now) residential segregation made distinguishing schools by students' social class easy to do. Most schools were predominantly one or another class.

That analysis gave me a simple choice of ways of organizing my material (which came from sixty interviews with teachers.) I could analyze, in turn, the relations teachers had with students, parents, principals, and other teachers, describing under each heading how those relations varied depending on the social class of the school. Or I could write in turn about slum schools, working-class schools, and upper middle–class schools, explaining the particular constellation of teachers' relations with those four groups that characterized schools of each class.

How did I choose? I couldn't see that it made any difference, at least with respect to the bulk of the writing I had to do. Whichever way I chose, I would have to describe teachers and working-class kids, teachers and slum school colleagues, teachers and the principals of middle-class schools, and all the other combinations of relations and school types created by cross-classifying relation and class. My smallest descriptive units, analyzing those combinations, would be the same. The opening and closing sentences, relating the smaller units to the whole, would be different, as would the final arguments I made. But I would be able to use whatever I wrote, however I finally put the material together. Either way, I would report the same results (although in a different order) and arrive at essentially the same conclusions (though the terms they were put in and their emphases would differ). What I said about the implications for social science theory and social policy would differ, naturally. If I used my results to answer different questions, the answers would look different. But none of that would affect the work that lay immediately ahead of me as I began writing my thesis. Why worry about it?

I worried about it—everyone worries about it—because the problem, while very important, can't be solved rationally. Whichever way I chose, I found myself wanting to talk about, or actually talking about, something I hadn't mentioned or explained yet. I could start by talking about slum schools, but only if I talked about the four groups and teachers' relations with them. But I couldn't talk about those relations without explaining the theoretical issues involved. I would have to explain, for instance, that service workers, like teachers, typically judge people they work with on the basis of how easy or difficult those people make it to get through a day's work. If I did that, I would be starting with the relations. But I couldn't say anything sensible about the relations without first explaining social class and its bearing on children's ability to learn school materials and to behave in ways acceptable to teachers, and on parents' willingness and ability to help teachers keep children in line. You can see where that leads.

It once led my colleague Blanche Geer to wish for a way to write what she had to say on the surface of a sphere, so that nothing would have to come first. That would shift the problem of what to take up first to the reader. The image of writing on a sphere exactly captures the insoluble nature of the problem, as people usually define it. You can't talk about everything at once, no matter how much you want to, no matter how much it seems to be the only way. You can, of course, solve the problem. Everyone eventually does. You do it by taking up, for instance, the relations between the teachers and other groups and saying that there is also this other way of looking at it, and in due time you will explain that too. This is not so much a placeholder as an IOU.

Writers find the question of how to organize a problem, again, because they imagine that one of the ways is right. They don't let themselves see that each of the several ways they can think of has something to recommend it, that none are perfect. Believers in Platonic perfection don't like pragmatic compromises and accept them only when reality—the need to finish a paper or thesis, for instance—compels it.

But writers have more immediate reasons to worry than not knowing the One Right Way. They don't even know, at the beginning, what those smallest units are, the fragments out of which the final result will be made. Another is that they don't have much idea about the alternate ways they might be put together. They don't, for instance, know that they can choose between organizing their discussion around kinds of schools or kinds of work relations. They have vague notions that one thing might lead to another, that one idea might stand in a causal relation of some sort to another, that one idea is a specific version of another more general one. But they might be wrong. Those ideas might contradict something they read in Durkheim or Weber, conflict with the results of someone else's research, or even be belied by their own data. People hope to solve these problems by making outlines.

Outlines can help, but not if you begin with them. If you begin, instead, by writing down everything, by spewing out your ideas as fast as you can type, you will discover the answer to the first question: the fragments you have to work with are the various things you have just written. These fragments will be at every level of generality or should be. Some will be specific observations: teachers hate kids who talk dirty. Some will be more general: teachers can't stand anyone challenging their authority in the classroom. Some will relate to the scholarly literature: Max Weber says that bureaucracy is a rule of secret sessions. Some will be about social organization: slum schools have unstable teacher populations, while upper-middle class schools, because teachers seldom leave them, have more stable teaching staffs.

Some will be about careers and individual experience: teachers who, for whatever reason, have spent several years in a slum school, no longer want to leave it.

Once you have the fragments, you can see how disparate they are, how they range from the general to the particular and don't seem to stick to any one way of thinking about your topic. Now you have to arrange them so that they at least seem to move logically from point to point in what a reader would recognize as a reasonable argument. How can you do that?

People solve this problem in a variety of ways. I use this principle to choose among possible solutions: Do whatever comes easiest first. Write the part that is easiest to write. Do simple housekeeping chores like sorting your papers out. That's an easy way to find out how to organize your materials. Its greatest virtue (which follows from the principle of doing easy things first) makes a difficult mental task into a largely physical, and therefore easier, one.

When I began this mode of analysis no computers or computer applications existed to help me get it done. I did it with file cards, which contained single ideas and the analysis proceeded by doing all the jobs I'm going to describe. Once those machines and applications did exist, I got rid of the physical apparatus, the file cards, because a text file could store my ideas and used use an outlining program. This task can now be done by most word processors, but I've always preferred an application custom made for the job. (My current long-time favorite is called *Opal* and if you can't find it by googling the word it's probably disappeared, but there are others. Look and you'll find one.)

These applications generally work like this. You type a phrase or sentence, and that starts a "topic." You type another sentence—an idea or an example, for instance—and indicate its logical connection to the first topic by where you put it on the screen: a continuation of the first sentence, easily indicated by continuing to type following the first one; a new topic, coordinated logically with the first one, placed directly below the first topic by hitting return; or a topic subordinate to the previous one, which you place, using ordinary typing commands, below and to the right of the previous topic, indicating an example or an extension of the previous topic. When you change the job the topic is doing in the flow of the argument, you indicate that by moving the topic to a place that indicates spatially the logical job it is doing (extension, example, etc.).

Using such a program, you begin the analysis by taking notes on what you've already written, putting each idea in an appropriate place on the screen. Don't throw away any of the ideas contained in your notes since they might come in handy, even if you don't see how at the moment. As you continue to type in the notes, arrange them under whatever topics and subtopics seem relevant to you, generating these labels as you go along and thereby actually beginning your analysis, but disguising it as the less serious and therefore less scary job of just copying your notes. This more or less "analyzes" your scattered ideas, putting the ones that seem to go together under the same heading in your growing outline. "Seem to go together?" Yes, and don't look too closely, for the moment, for what they have in common. Follow your intuition.

Once you've assembled these topics with their casually constructed but nevertheless logical organization, make sure that the major topic under which others are gathered really summarizes what all the entries beneath it say, generalizing their particulars. That's how you find the more general idea they've been harboring. The physical sorting you create with the computer commands generates it. But now you find out that some of the items placed under your major heading, your general idea, don't fit. No problem. Take them out and put them somewhere else, creating a new idea/topic for them if that's what it takes.

You'll soon see that there is more than one way, but not very many more, to make your case. The ways aren't identical, because they emphasize different parts of your analysis. If I organize my analysis of schoolteachers around kinds of schools, I will emphasize the local social organization of the school, to some degree losing the comparative emphasis on professional problems an analysis focused on the relations would emphasize.

Doing all these things, by the way, helps solve another common "minor" problem. Social scientists reporting empirical research always include a descriptive section, telling something about the country, town, or organization they did their research in. What should such sections include? Researchers vaguely intend them to give readers "a feel for the place," and fill them from a commonly accepted list of things every reader would presumably need (or at least) want to know, a mélange of geography, demography, history, and organization charts.

Creating the outline of your argument this way helps you make these choices more rationally, because these facts about places, people, and organizations give readers more than a general familiarity. Social organizations work the way research reports say they do only with the right kinds of people in the right kinds of places. So preliminary descriptive materials set down some of the basic premises, often unstated, the report's argument rests on. If our book (Becker, Geer, and Hughes 1968, 15 ff.) describes a college student culture which profoundly affects student lives and perspectives, the reader wants, not unreasonably, to know that the college we are talking about is, as was the case for us, large and is, in fact, the dominant institution in a small midwestern town, and that a large number of the students come from smaller, less cosmopolitan places.

There's one further way of dealing with organizational problems. Instead of trying to solve the insoluble, you can talk about it. You can explain to readers why whatever it is is a problem, what ways of solving it you have thought about, why you chose the less-than-perfect solution you actually chose, and what it all means. The what-it-all-means will be interesting because you wouldn't be having the problem if it didn't embody some interesting dilemma in the work you are doing—for instance, the way problems of class and professional structure intersect in concrete organizations so that you can't talk about class without talking about teachers' shared perspectives on their professional relations, and can't talk about those without talking about class. You have trouble only if you insist that, in principle, they have to be discussable separately.

Discussing them, instead of trying to wish them away, solves all sorts of scientific problems, not just writing problems. When anthropologists and sociologists do field research, for instance, they typically have problems establishing and maintaining relationships with people that will let them observe what they want to over a long period of time. Delays and obstructions while you negotiate these arrangements can be discouraging. But experienced fieldworkers know that the difficulties provide valuable clues to the social organization they want to understand. How people respond to a stranger who wants to study them reveals something about how their lives are organized. If the poor people in a city neighborhood you want to study are suspicious and won't talk to you, that's a real problem. You may eventually discover that they are standoffish because they think you might be an investigator trying to catch violators of welfare regulations. The trouble, personally painful, will have taught you something worth knowing.

Similarly, experimental social psychologists got upset when published work demonstrated that an experimenter's seemingly extraneous and irrelevant actions affected the results of experiments independently of the variables investigators supposed were at work. They shouldn't have. As Rosenthal showed (1966), while psychologists thus lost the illusion of total control over experimental situations, they gained a new and interesting area of study: social influence in small groups. They gained that by talking about their insoluble problem rather than ignoring it.

It's the same with writing. When you can't find the One Right Way to say it, talk about why you can't. Bennett Berger adopted this solution in *The Survival of a Counterculture* (1981), which reported his study of hippie communes in northern California. He was interested in utopian experiments. He felt personally close to the hippie culture and ethos. He wanted to study how communards handled the inevitable gap between what they professed and how they behaved as they adapted their beliefs to the circumstances of their lives. He called the methods people used to address those gaps "ideological work" and conceived of studying such work as a microsociology of knowledge. But he had trouble writing about what he found:

> I delayed writing this book for several years because I couldn't find an interpretive frame to put around the social life I observed. Without that frame, I wasn't sure that I understood the meaning of what I was seeing. Without that understanding, I had no posture toward the data, and that reduced my motivation to write. And when that understanding emerged, I didn't like the "cynical" posture it invited me to take. (xxi)

He described the problem of the cynical posture, which bothered him deeply, as it affected the study he had done in the commune:

> [It is] the tendency of the sociology of knowledge to impugn, weaken, or undermine ideas when analysis of them reveals their self-and group-serving functions. . . . If the idea of urban apocalypse serves the interests of survival-equipped communards, is that sufficient reason for casting a cold and skeptical eye on it? If the idea of equal rights for children serves the purpose of those adults who initially had neither the time nor the inclination to be middle-class parents, is that sufficient reason for being cynical about their motives? If the affirmation of "authenticity" in interpersonal relationships serves the interests of people so situated that their dense interactional textures make them ill-able to afford emotional disguises, isn't that reason to regard [their belief in] "openness 'n honesty" as simply another self-serving element of ideology (like belief in cultural pluralism by ethnic minorities or in low taxes by the wealthy)? Or on the other hand, when groups are caught in contradictions between the ideas they profess to believe in and their day-to-day behavior, is their hurried ideological repair work best understood in an ironic, contemptuous, and cynical manner?
> My answer to these questions is no, at least insofar as

the [people he studied] dealt with them. But the answers provided by the major tradition of the sociology of knowledge would seem to be a resounding YES—in part because one of the major motives informing the sociology of knowledge as an intellectual enterprise has been the desire to "unmask" or "demystify" ideas by revealing the "real" interests or functions they serve. (168–69)

"It's easy to see how such a problem can paralyze you: It has taken me a long time to gain the perspective on beliefs and circumstances adopted in this book, and my failure to apprehend it earlier has functioned as a kind of bit in my mouth, preventing me from speaking clearly" (223). Berger wanted to discuss the social bases of what communards believed without making fun of or looking down on them. Until he could figure out how to do that, he couldn't write his book. I don't want to pursue his argument further (although it deserves to be read in full) because I am citing it as a solution to another kind of problem— not Berger's problem of how to avoid making fun of what he was studying, but the even more common difficulty of not being able to write because you haven't found the One Right Way to handle that or some other problem. Berger doesn't say how to avoid that fruitless search for the One Right Way, but he demonstrates how. Write about it. Make it the focus of your analysis. He devoted a sizeable part of his book to just that task. In so doing, he found a way to write his book as well as a large subject to embed the story of his research in: the intellectual vice of explanation as a putdown.

Taking readers into your confidence about your troubles requires admitting that you had them and, therefore, that you are not the paragon who always knows the Right Way and executes it flawlessly. I don't think that difficult, since no such paragons exist, but some people don't like to make such admissions. The remedy is to try it and prove to yourself that it doesn't hurt.

4 : Editing by Ear

When I edit people's work, or talk about editing to them, they usually want to know (as Rosanna did) what the principles of editing are. What rules do I use to decide, for instance, when to leave a word out or delete a phrase? No one does anything creative by merely following rules (although rules are necessary and helpful), and even the most routine and trivial writing is creative, whether it's a letter to a friend or a note to a delivery person. Unless you are copying a form letter out of a book or writing the fiftieth thank-you note in exactly the words you used for the other forty-nine, you are creating new language, new combinations, something that didn't exist until you put it down that way.

Grammarians and composition teachers recommend several kinds of rules and guidelines. Many rules, like those requiring that a declarative sentence end with a period or that writing proceed from left to right, do what conventions typically do in the arts: make it possible to communicate a thought by providing a minimum of shared understanding between creator and consumer.

Other rules make it possible to communicate with less chance of unintended confusion and misunderstanding: rules requiring that pronouns agree with their antecedents, for instance. Still others are not rules at all, but rather guidelines to conventional usage and precise meaning (like distinguishing between *reticent* and *reluctant*). Some, finally, are truly matters of taste, about which reasonable people differ, usually along conservative-progressive lines: Should I have used the word "bullshit" in chapter 1?

What role do these rules and guidelines play in the creation of a piece of writing? It might work like this: we put down whatever comes into our heads, then go back over the result with a rule book in hand, find all the violations of rules, and bring the text into line with the rule book. Isn't that what we do when we rewrite?

No. We might do something a little like that, but bringing the text into line with the rule book can't be that automatic. Bringing it into line is creative too. Furthermore, sociologists' studies of obedience to rules show that rules are never so clear and unambiguous that we can simply follow them. We always have to decide whether a rule exists at all, whether what we have is really covered by the rule, or whether there might not be some exception that isn't in the book but one the rule makers, we think, must have intended. We also need to interpret rules so that the result we get is reasonable, not some foolishness resulting from blind rule following. (Harold Garfinkel [1967, 21–24] describes this practice, which he calls ad hocing, as a fundamental feature of all human activity.)

Mike Rose, drawing on his experience advising students with writer's block, distinguishes two kinds of rules, one clearly better suited to the activity of rewriting:

Algorithms are precise rules that will always result in a specific answer if applied to an appropriate problem. Most mathematical rules, for example, are algorithms. Functions are constant (e.g., pi), procedures are routine (squaring the radius), and outcomes are completely predictable. However, few day-to-day situations are mathematically circumscribed enough to warrant the application of algorithms. Most often we function with the aid of fairly general heuristics or "rules of thumb," guidelines that allow varying degrees of flexibility when approaching problems. Rather than operating with algorithmic precision and certainty, we search, critically, through alternatives, using our heuristic as a divining rod—"if a math problem stumps you, try working backwards to solution"; "if the car won't start, check x, y, or z," and so forth. Heuristics won't allow the precision or the certitude afforded by algorithmic operations; heuristics can even be so "loose" as to be vague. But in a world where tasks and problems are rarely mathematically precise, heuristic rules become the most appropriate, the most functional rules available to us. (Rose 1983, 391–92)

Not surprisingly, students who thought rules about writing were algorithms (I'm not inventing straw men—some did) had trouble, while students who used them as heuristics didn't.

We can't, then, write or even rewrite by treating whatever rules we might decide on as algorithms. If not that way, how? We do it by ear. What does that mean? Looking at a blank sheet of paper, or one with writing on it, we use what "sounds good" or "looks good" to us. We use heuristics, some precise, some quite vague.

Most of the time, when social scientists write, they don't think about rules or guidelines at all. Although they don't consult a rule book, they do consult something: a standard of taste, a generalized notion of what something ought to look or sound like. If the result doesn't conflict too much with that generalized picture they let it stand. They work, in other words, like artists, who

often find it difficult to verbalize the general principles on which they make their choices, or even to give any reasons at all. They often resort to such noncommunicative statements as "it sounds better that way," "it looked good to me," or "it works."

That inarticulateness frustrates the researcher. But every art's [read "academic discipline's"] practitioners use words whose meanings they cannot define exactly which are nevertheless intelligible to all knowledgeable members of their worlds. Jazz musicians say that something does or does not "swing"; theater people say that a scene "works" or does not "work." In neither case can even the most knowledgeable participant explain to someone not already familiar with the terms' uses what they mean. Yet everyone who uses them understands them and can apply them with great reliability, agreeing about what swings or works, even though they cannot say what they mean.

[This] suggests that they do not work by consulting a set of rules or criteria. Rather, they respond as they imagine others might respond, and construct those imaginings from their repeated experiences of hearing people apply the undefined terms in concrete situations. (Becker 1982a, 199–200)

Sociologists' standards of taste do include rules they learned in composition classes, which they have trained themselves to apply almost automatically. I habitually scan almost anything I read for passive constructions; if it is my prose, I immediately consider whether and how to change them. I am not aware of applying a rule or heuristic and don't consult a book to know when or how to do it. But I know what I am doing and can state the relevant principle if asked (as I did for Rosanna). Most sociologists use some such rules, many of which unfortunately work as unanalyzed algorithmic stumbling blocks rather than aids.

Most sociologists, however, have few consciously formulated heuristics. More often, they rely on the fallible and uninspected judgments of their ear. They develop that ear, their standards of prose, mainly from what they read. They read work they admire and want what they write to resemble it, to look that way on the page. That probably explains why scholarly writing so often deteriorates as students move through graduate school and into an academic career. They read the professional journals and want their work to look like what they read, for reasons I've already discussed. That suggests an immediate remedy for bad academic writing: read outside your professional field, and when you do, choose good models.

We are not stuck forever with the standard of taste we acquired when we entered our discipline. In fact, we change it considerably, even in the short run. We develop our taste not only from reading, but also from what our friends and peers say to us or what we fear they might say. A colleague of mine feared, when he wrote, the unlikely possibility that his prose would end up at the bottom of a New Yorker column as a hideous example of academic writing. Such fears can move a sensitive victim to study a book on style in order to incorporate the heuristics they recommend into his or her standard of taste.

But most sociologists (and probably most academic writers) don't hear many critical remarks about their prose or, if they do, don't hear them from anyone they have to pay attention to. Since ignoring problems of writing causes them no immediate and obvious trouble, they spend their time on statistics and methods and theory, which can and do cause problems. Editors and professors reject papers that use statistics incorrectly, but only sigh over those badly written. Because content matters more to a field's progress than style, professors will not flunk smart students who write badly, and some highly esteemed sociologists were notoriously incomprehensible.

The spectacle of a field which cares so little for decent prose may shock outsiders as much it tires insiders, but that is sociology (and probably many other scholarly disciplines), as it has been for many years and continuing to be well into the twenty-first century. As a result, young sociologists have no reason to learn any more about writing than they knew when they began graduate school, and will probably lose some of the skills they do have. If their college English classes haven't given them a standard of taste that includes, as working rules, the elements of grammar and style, they won't spend the time to study them seriously. So they will learn to do their editing by ear, if they learn to do it at all.

Since I learned what little I know about writing and editing that way, fortuitously and haphazardly, I find it hard to produce general editorial principles on request. I can, however, give examples, preferably from the work of the person asking the question, and suggest general ideas that seem to be relevant to their problems. Of course, these notions can't be stated algorithmically. I can't say that you must never use passive constructions, but I can say that a particular passive construction misstates an important sociological idea. Nor is it always wrong to use long, abstract words. I have nevertheless, later in this chapter, stated such rules dogmatically because, while passive constructions are sometimes useful, sociologists do not need to be advised to use them, or long, abstract words either. They do those things automatically.

What follow are some examples of how I edit, with some discussion of the choices made, the reasoning behind them, and the guidelines those choices imply. This will put some more flesh on the prescriptions I gave my class. The examples come from early drafts of an article I wrote on photography (Becker 1982b; the published version differs from that quoted here.) The examples are not remarkable; I can find their like in anything I have ever written and in much that I have published.

To begin, consider the following paragraph, which discusses the strategy of describing social groups through photographic portraits of their members:

Whatever part they [photographers] let stand for the person, the strategy implies a theory and a method. The theory is a simple one, but it is important to make its steps explicit, so that we can see how it works. The theory is that the life a person has lived, its good times and bad, leaves its marks. Someone who has lived a happy life will have a face that shows that. Someone who has managed to maintain their human dignity in the face of trouble will have a face that shows that. . . . This is a daring strategy, because it makes the little that the photograph does contain carry an enormous weight. We must, if the theory is to work and help us to produce effective images, choose faces, details of them, and moments in their history which, recorded on film and printed on paper, allow viewers to infer everything else they are interested in. Viewers, that is, look at the lines on a face and infer from them a life spent in hard work in the sun.

When I began rewriting this passage, the phrase "it is import-ant to," in the second sentence, caught my attention as typical throat clearing. If it's important to do it, don't talk about it, *do it*. (This is a typical guideline which is by no means a rule.) I first changed "it is important to" to "we need to." That made the sentence more active, and slightly stronger, and introduced an agent, someone actually doing it. Things that are not done by anyone, but "just are," have a fuzzy quality I don't like.

Having made that change, I still wasn't happy. The sentence had three clauses which were just strung together. If I can re-arrange a sentence so that its organization displays and thus reinforces the connections I am describing, I do. So I cut the first clause, putting its content into an adjectival phrase. Instead of saying the theory was a simple one, I replaced "its steps" in the second clause with "the steps of this simple theory." A few words less, and the simplicity of the theory reduced to a small descrip-tive point: "We need to make the steps of this simple theory ex-plicit. . . ." Having done it, I no longer had to say that we needed to do it, which was no better than saying it was important to do it. The rewritten sentence reads, "If we make the steps of this simple theory explicit, we can see how it works." It has sixteen words instead of twenty-three. The three strung-together clauses now make an if-then argument that is more interesting than the list it replaced.

Now look at the fourth sentence. I changed "Someone" to "People" for no very good reason, mainly because I wanted to get at "managed to maintain." Wordy phrases like "manage to maintain" try to make simple statements sound profound. Talking about people's ability to act evokes the academic urge to profundity. It seems trivial to say that people "can" do something. We prefer to say that they "had the capability of" or "the ability to" or even, striving for simplicity, that they "were able to." I almost invariably use such constructions in early drafts and replace them with "can" when I rewrite. So I changed the sentence to "People who have kept . . ."

Finally, consider the sentence about lines on a face: "Viewers, that is, look at the lines on a face and infer from them a life spent in hard work in the sun." I cut some words that weren't doing much work. I proved that "that is" was meaningless *by* taking it out and seeing that the sentence lost no meaning. Applying the same test, I changed "a life spent in hard work" to a "life of hard work." But I also saw a way to add a few words and make the image more concrete: "Viewers look at the lines on a face and infer that they were baked in during a life of hard work in the sun." A slight transposition remedies the ambiguity of "they" and reads even better: "Looking at the lines on a face, viewers infer that . . ."

The final version, as published, went like this:

Whatever part a photographer chooses to stand for the person, he or she is employing a strategy that relies on a theory and a method. This strategy depends on the assumption that the experiences of life are recorded in faces, that the life a person has lived leaves physical marks.

Photographers, accordingly, choose faces, details of faces, and moments in their histories which, recorded on film and printed on paper, allow viewers to deduce what they don't see but want to know about. Portraits often contain a wealth of detail, so that careful study allows us to make complex and subtle readings of the character of the person and of the life-in-society of that person. Looking at the lines on a face, viewers may conclude that that these were baked in during a life of hard work in the sun. From these same lines, they can infer wisdom produced by hard work and age or, alternatively, senility and decay. To make any of these conclusions, a viewer must bring to bear on the image one of several possible theories of facial lines.

That doesn't exhaust what might be done here.

Two sentences, further on in the article, combined several common difficulties. I gave an example of how a well-known contemporary photographed the interiors of buildings with people in them: "Some of Robert Frank's most compelling images are of offices after hours, with no one there—no one but the janitor cleaning up. A bank looks different when it is occupied by a janitor than when it is occupied by bankers."

I might almost leave this, in the style of a mathematics text, as an exercise for the reader to repair. Not to be a tease about it, however, I began by stating the first phrase more actively: "Robert Frank made some of his most compelling images. . . ." That let me rearrange and simplify the next construction: "Robert Frank made some of his most compelling images in offices after hours," and went on, cutting a repetition I thought forceful when I first wrote it, "when no one was there but the janitors." Why did I cut the "cleaning up" that followed "janitors"? Because I now meant to put that thought into a more concrete image in the next sentence, which I changed to: "A bank occupied only by a janitor pushing a mop looks different from one filled with bankers on the phone." That let me contrast the bankers' telephoning and the janitors' mop-pushing, rather than just mentioning their job titles and letting the reader fill in their characteristic actions. The rewritten sentence also eliminates the repetition of something being "occupied by" somebody. Saying that bankers "filled" the space emphasized the contrast between the bustle of daytime business and the quiet of night-time cleaning that Frank's photograph called attention to.

Here are some further short illustrations. I changed "If you do the former [there is no point in explaining the specifics of these examples], you may be able to" to "The former lets you."

I changed "Older houses have lots of [if I had said, less colloqui-ally, "many," it wouldn't have made any difference] rooms with doors on them" to "The rooms in older houses have doors on them." (And now, after publication, I realize that I should have deleted "on them" too.) I changed "according to the method just described" to "by the method just described" and "the change that has occurred in conceptions of privacy" to "the change in conceptions of privacy."

We spent a lot of time in my writing seminar making similar changes in specimens donated by friends, colleagues, and even-tually the students themselves. Students found it difficult at first to understand why, having rewritten a sentence, I then rewrote it again, and even a third or fourth time. Why didn't I get it right the first time? I said, and tried to show them, that each change opened the way to other changes, that when you cleared away nonworking words and phrases, you could see more easily what the sentence was about and could phrase it more succinctly and accurately.

They also wondered if picking away at such tiny matters of wording really affected the result. They found the exercise te-dious at first, and to be truthful, I prolonged the first session un-forgivably. I wanted them to see that there was always something more to discuss, some further possible change; that I could and probably would question every word and punctuation mark; and that they should learn to do likewise. They found the exercise un-nerving. They could not imagine raising all those questions about every sentence. Eventually I reassured them, as their own expe-rience does eventually. They discovered that the process doesn't take as much time as they feared, that you could quickly spot the obvious problems and needed to worry only about a few that are truly difficult to solve. They learned that line-by-line editing is easy because the things to fix fall into classes. When you under-stand the nature of a class, you know how to fix the problems of the sentences that belong to it. (This was, I guess, my way of talking to them about rules and guidelines.)

What the students accepted less easily was worth doing. They could see that each change made things marginally clearer and cut out a few words that probably weren't doing much work anyway. But what good was that? I know that when I finished *Art Worlds*, I thought I had done all the editing the prose needed or could stand. A gifted copyeditor, Helen Tartar, went over it and made hundreds of further changes, few as extensive as the ones I just described. When I read the material with her changes, I felt the way I do when, looking through the viewfinder of my camera, I give the lens that last quarter turn that brings everything into perfect focus. Good editing does that, and it's worth doing. The unnecessary words take up room and are thus uneconomic. They cheat, demanding attention by hinting at profundities and sophistication they don't deliver. Seeming to mean something, those extra words mislead readers about what is being said.

The sentences we just considered exemplify classes of problems and the way the problems can be solved. None of the guidelines I am going to give is original. It would be a wonder if they were. Generations of English teachers, editors, and writers have discovered and rediscovered them, taught them to students, and recommended them to writers. Some word-processing programs even look for typical stylistic faults and suggest corrections. I don't trust them well enough to leave the job to them. You can if you want to, but don't say I didn't warn you! Here's my version, tailored to the needs of sociologists, but perhaps useful to scholars in other disciplines as well.

1. *Active/passive.* Every writing text wants you to substitute active verbs for passive ones when you can. (Doesn't that sound better than saying "The necessity of replacing passive verbs with active ones is emphasized in every book on writing"?) What matters more than the grammatical distinction between active and passive is the simple act of putting the crucial actions into verbs and making some important character in the story you are telling the subject of the verb. But paying attention to the grammatical distinction starts you on the right road. Active verbs almost always force you to name the person (or organization, etc.) who did whatever was done (although gifted obfuscators can avoid

the requirement). We seldom think that things just happen all by themselves, as passive verbs suggest, because in our daily lives people do things and *make them happen*. Sentences that name active agents make our representations of social life more understandable and believable. "The criminal was sentenced" hides the judge who, we know, did the sentencing and, not incidentally, thus makes the criminal's fate seem the operation of impersonal forces rather than the result of people acting together to imprison him or her. Almost every version of social theory insists that we *act* to produce social life. Karl Marx and George Herbert Mead both thought that, but their followers' syntax often betrays the theory.

2. *Fewer words.* Scholarly writers often insert words and whole phrases when they don't want to say something as flatly as it first came to them. They want to indicate a modesty, a reservation, a sense that they know they might be wrong. Sometimes they want to recognize that readers may disagree by suggesting politely, before actually saying whatever they are going to say, that it "merits attention," instead of just saying it right out, as though it of course merited attention. That's why I had said at first "it was important" to make the theory's steps explicit. But if it isn't important, why bother to do it? And if it is, won't doing it make that clear enough without a preliminary announcement?

We scholars also use unnecessary words because we think, like the student in my seminar, that if we say it plainly it will sound like something anybody could say rather than the profound statement only a social scientist could make. We give it that special importance by suggesting that some important process underlies what we are talking about. So I had at first spoken of people who "managed to maintain" their dignity. That hints, as "people who have kept" their dignity doesn't, that keeping their dignity was difficult and they had to work at it. But I was writing about photographers, not about people surmounting trouble. While people do *maintain* their dignity, just as the phrase suggests, this article doesn't talk about that, and it was therefore distracting and pointless to mention it. Similarly, "the change *that has occurred* in conceptions of privacy" makes the process of change in those conceptions important. If I delete the italicized words, the point I want to make is intact and I have removed a distracting reference to an unanalyzed process I won't mention again.

Sometimes we put those throat-clearing phrases in because the rhythm or structure of the sentence seems to require it, or because we want to remind ourselves that something is missing in the argument. We want to make an if-then argument, but we haven't consciously worked out the causal connection our intuition thinks is there. So we make the form and hope the content will appear to fill it. Or we do it out of habit. We get attached to locutions and formats. Like many scholarly writers, I often write sentences with three predicate clauses: "This book excites our curiosity, gives us some answers, and convinces us that the author is right." (The second sentence of the next paragraph is another good example, one that occurred naturally as I was writing.) But I often use that form whether I have three things to say or not, and then I have to scratch for the third thing, which is then vacuous. No harm. It comes out in editing.

An unnecessary word does no work. It doesn't further an argument, state an important qualification, or add a compelling detail. (See?) I find unnecessary words by a simple test. As I read through my draft, I check each word and phrase to see what happens if I remove it. If the meaning doesn't change, I take it out. The deletion often makes me see what I really wanted there, and I put it in. I seldom take unnecessary words out of early drafts. I'll see them when I rewrite and either replace them with working words or cut them.

3. *Repetition.* Scholars create some of their most impenetrable obscurities by trying to be clear. They know that vague pronouns and ambiguous syntax can leave what they mean unclear, so they repeat words and phrases if there is any possibility of confusion. That may not confuse readers, but it usually bores them. I am not simply repeating the mechanical rule we all learned in high school: don't repeat the same word within so-and-so many sen-

tences. You may have to repeat words, but you shouldn't repeat words when you can get the same result without doing it. Remember my sentence: "A bank looks different when it is occupied by a janitor than when it is occupied by bankers." "When it is occupied" doesn't require repetition and makes readers' minds wander. If I think about it, I can create a more compact and interesting sentence, as I tried to do in that example.

4. *Structure/content*. The thoughts a sentence conveys usually have a logical structure, stating or implying some sort of connection between the things it discusses. We might want to say that something resembles or actually is something else (state an identity): "A mental hospital is a total institution." We might want to describe an identifying characteristic of a class of phenomena: "People who move from the country are marginal to the urban society they enter." We might want to identify something as a member of a class: "Monet was an Impressionist." We might want to state a causal connection or an if-then relation: "Slums produce crime" or "If a child grows up in a broken home, that child will become delinquent." We can state these connections as I have just done. That will be enough to make our point clear. But we can be even clearer by reinforcing the point syntactically.

Syntax, the way we arrange the sentence's elements, indicates the relations between them. We can reinforce a sentence's thought by arranging its elements so that its syntax *also* makes the argument or, at least, does not interfere with the reader understanding it. We can, for example, put subordinate thoughts in subordinate positions in the sentence. If we put them in positions of importance, readers will think they are important. If we make every thought in the sentence equally important grammatically by stringing together coordinate clauses, readers will think they are equally important. That happens when, giving in to habit, I say I have three things to discuss and then label them one, two, and three or just list them one after the other. We can usually make our point more forcefully by going from one to the next in a way that shows how they are connected other than by following one another in a list.

5. *Concrete/abstract.* Scholars generally, and sociologists particularly, use far too many abstract words. Sometimes we use abstractions because we don't have anything very specific in mind. Scholars have favorite abstract words which act as placeholders. Meaning nothing in themselves, they mark a place that needs a real idea. Complex or complicated and relation exemplify the type. We say that there is a complex relation between two things. What have we said? "Relation" is such a general concept that it means almost nothing, which is why it is so useful in very abstract branches of mathematics. All it says is that two things are connected somehow. But almost any two things are related *somehow.* In disciplines less abstract than mathematics we usually want to know *how.* That's what's worth knowing. Complex doesn't tell us, it just says, "Believe me, there's a lot to it," which most people would concede about almost anything. Most of the spatial metaphors used in discussions of social life and other scholarly topics—levels and positions in social organizations, for instance—cheat readers of concrete specificity that way. So do phrases which hint that what we are describing is part of a collection of similar things: "a set of" or "a kind of."

We also use abstractions to indicate the general application of our thought. We don't want anyone to think that what we found out is only true of Chicago schoolteachers or a mental hospital in Washington DC. We want them to understand that what we found where we did our research can be found under similar circumstances anywhere in the world, any time in history. There is nothing wrong with that: it's a major reason for doing sociological research. We can best convince readers of the generality of our results by describing what we have studied in specific detail and then showing, in similar detail, what class of things it belongs to and what other things are likely to belong to that class. If I show in detail how people learn to smoke marijuana from others and how that affects their experience of the drug's effects, I can go on to describe a class of similar phenomena in similar specificity: how people learn from others to understand their inner physical experiences. The specific case I have described in detail provides a model to which readers can refer my more general ideas. Without the specifics, the general ideas don't mean much.

Writing manuals tell us to use concrete details because they make the matter more alive to the reader, more memorable. Williams (1981), for instance, says: "Regardless of our audience, we can make writing readable and memorable by writing specifically and concretely. When we squeeze long, windy phrases into more compact phrases, we make diffuse ideas sharply specific. . . . The more narrow the reference, the more concrete the idea; the more concrete the idea, the clearer and more precise the idea" (132–33).

When we use concrete details to give body to abstractions, however, we should choose the details and examples carefully. The example that readers have in mind will bring in considerations not explicitly addressed in the general argument and color our understanding of it. Kathryin Pyne Addelson, a philosopher, criticized the philosophical analysis of abortion by noting that their authors typically concoct very fanciful examples—of hypothetical women impregnated by flying insects and the like—and that such a choice of examples lets them reach conclusions they would not support if they discussed the case of a pregnant forty-year old woman with five children whose husband is out of work.

6. *Metaphors.* If you have leafed through any academic journal in the past fifty years, you have found on almost every page trite metaphorical talk. Here are some I collected when I wrote the first edition of this book and, though the metaphors may have changed, the amount of metaphorical deadwood won't have changed much: "Some cutting edge seems lacking" in a book being reviewed. Another book "covers a huge terrain." A third deals with "a rich issue that has been impoverished by its context." My colleagues talked about "the growing body of literature," analyses that "penetrate to the heart" of the problem being discussed or "fall between two stools," and find "the seeds" of another society's institutional practices "planted in our own society." A theoretical approach leads to a "conceptual straitjacket." Researchers "mine" data or "ferret" or "tease" results out of them and get to

"the bottom line." The most scientific document contains a lot of such metaphorical talk.

I usually cut such metaphors out of anything I am editing. All metaphors? No, only ones like the above. You can see their kind by comparing them to a masterful use of metaphor, Goffman's (1952) justly well-known paper "On Cooling the Mark Out," which uses the criminal confidence game as a metaphor for those social situations in which someone cannot sustain the definition of self they have offered to themselves and the world. I would leave that metaphor in anything I edited.

The difference between the two kinds of metaphor lies in the seriousness and attention with which they are used. I don't mean how seriously authors take their subject, but how seriously they take the details of their metaphor. Goffman took the con game metaphor seriously. He compared the other situations he analyzed—the lover whose proposal is rejected, the big shot who can't get a table in a crowded restaurant, the person who can't manage the ordinary routines of everyday life well enough to avoid drawing attention to himself—to the con game point for point. In particular, he noted that the marks who lost their money to confidence men realized (and supposed that others would also see) that they were not nearly as smart as they had thought when they tried to get rich quick. Criminal tradition suggested to con men that they could avoid trouble by helping the angry victims restore their self-esteem, by "cooling them out." So con men routinely assigned a team member to use well-established methods for achieving that result. Goffman used the metaphor to discover and describe the same job and the same role in restaurants and other places where people were likely to be so exposed, and even suggested that, since some people suffered such exposure in many areas of life, we could probably find professionals who handled such problems in a more general way. He identified psychiatry as a discipline devoted to cooling out people whose pretensions social life had unveiled as unrealistic. That discovery validated the metaphor for many readers. But the metaphor validated itself by being serious, by *meaning* that these other situations were like the con game in all sorts of ways, large and small.

The earlier metaphors I quoted from sociology journals weren't serious about their ramifications. When we say an argument has a "cutting edge," what tool are we comparing it to and what material is it supposed to be cutting? Who "covers terrain" in real life, how do they cover it, and what are the problems of terrain covering? Is the literature being compared to a human body? Does that mean we should look for its heart, its liver, its stomach, its brain? The authors never meant us to take their metaphors that seriously. The comparisons these "tired metaphors" make no longer live in the minds of those who write them or read them.

A metaphor that works is still alive. Reading it shows you a new aspect of what you are reading about, how that aspect appears in something that, on the surface, seems quite different. Using a metaphor is a serious theoretical exercise which asserts that two different empirical phenomena belong to the same general class, and general classes always imply a theory. But metaphors work that way only if they are fresh enough to attract attention. If they have been used repeatedly enough to be clichés, you don't see anything new. In fact, you think that they actually mean, literally, what they allude to metaphorically. Take the common expression, "to take the wind out of someone's sails." I had used that, read it, and heard it for years, but it never meant any more to me than that you somehow deflated the person you did it to. Then I learned to sail. In sailing races, your opponents try to come between you and the wind, so that their sail keeps the wind from hitting yours. When they do that successfully, your sails, full of wind and pushing you along briskly a moment before, suddenly begin to flap emptily. The hull's friction in the water, now that no wind is pushing to counteract it, brings the boat to a sudden halt. The metaphor came to life for me, recalling an irritating experience in all its fullness. But the metaphor means little or nothing to people who haven't had that experience.

All the tired metaphors once lived. As metaphors age, they lose their force from sheer repetition, so that they take up space but contribute less than a plain, nonmetaphorical statement. It is clearer and more pointed to say that a book's argument is diffuse than to say that "some cutting edge is lacking." If an author is lucky, no one pays any attention to the literal meaning of the metaphorical statement. When I read about "babies being thrown out with the bathwater," I still find it hard to keep a straight face. The same is true with "falling between two stools." What were those people trying to do with those stools, anyway?

Metaphors also deteriorate from misuse. People who don't know and understand the phenomenon well, who may really not know what they are talking about when they use the words, use them incorrectly, thinking they mean something else. The common metaphor of "the bottom line," for instance, refers to the bottom line of an accountant's report which, summarizing all the previous computations, lets you know , for instance, whether you made or lost money that year. Metaphorically, it could refer to the final result of any series of calculations: the population of the United States as discovered by the 2010 Census or the correlation between income and education in someone's study. But people often use it to indicate a final offer, the price they will not lower, the indignity they will not suffer: "That's the bottom line! I quit!" People who say that don't know, or don't remember, that the words have a financial referent. They probably use the expression because they like the air of finality "bottom" conveys, implying a point beyond which you can't go.

We can't, and shouldn't try to, avoid using another kind of metaphor, the ones permanently built into our language, which Lakoff and Johnson (1980) have analyzed in great detail. I'll give one example, of what they call

orientational metaphors, since most of them have to do with spatial orientation: up-down, in-out, front-back, on-off, deep-shallow, central-peripheral. These spatial orientations arise from the fact that we have bodies of the sort we have and that they function as they do in our physical environment. Orientational metaphors give a concept a spatial orientation; for example, HAPPY IS UP. The fact that the concept HAPPY is oriented UP leads to English expressions like "I'm feeling up today." (14)

Lakoff and Johnson go on to show how ubiquitously UP and DOWN and their relatives appear in our speech:

CONSCIOUS IS UP; UNCONSCIOUS IS DOWN
HEALTH AND LIFE ARE UP; SICKNESS AND DEATH ARE
    DOWN
HAVING CONTROL OR FORCE IS UP; BEING SUBJECT TO
    CONTROL OR FORCE IS DOWN
MORE IS UP; LESS IS DOWN
FORESEEABLE FUTURE EVENTS ARE UP (AND AHEAD)
HIGH STATUS IS UP; LOW STATUS IS DOWN
GOOD IS UP; BAD IS DOWN
VIRTUE IS UP; DEPRAVITY IS DOWN
RATIONAL IS UP; EMOTIONAL IS DOWN

Here is their analysis of the last example:

RATIONAL IS UP; EMOTIONAL IS DOWN
The discussion *fell to the emotional* level, but I *raised* it back *up to the rational* plane. We put our *feelings* aside and had a *high-level intellectual* discussion of the matter. He couldn't *rise above* his *emotions*.
    Physical and cultural basis: In our culture people view themselves as being in control over animals, plants, and their physical environment, and it is their unique ability to reason that places human beings above other animals and gives them this control. CONTROL IS UP thus provides a basis for MAN IS UP and therefore for RATIONAL IS UP. (17)

The book contains over two hundred pages of such analyses and examples. As I said, you can't avoid such metaphors. But being aware of them lets you use their overtones purposefully.

If you ignore the overtones your prose will fight with itself, the language conveying one idea, the metaphors another, and readers won't be sure what you mean.

This chapter barely touches what goes into creating a standard of taste that will let you edit your own work, and that of others, successfully. The main lesson is not the specifics of what I have said but the Zen lesson of *paying attention*. Writers need to pay close attention to what they have written as they revise, looking at every word as if they meant it to be taken seriously. You can write first drafts quickly and carelessly exactly because you know you will be critical later. When you pay close attention the problems start taking care of themselves.

And remember—we'll return to this later—editing by ear relies partly on your familiarity with current usage, knowing what will be understandable and meaningful to the audience reading what you write, either a narrowly professional audience or a more general one. Being alert to current standards in your field, on the one hand, tells you how your peers say things now, but also makes you vulnerable to meaning-deadening usages that may achieve some short-term goals you pay for in a loss of clarity, understandability and grace, which affect the longer-term interest of your work to a greater variety of readers. I'll return to these problems in a later chapter.

5 : Learning to Write as a Professional

Earlier chapters discussed how the institutions of scholarly life, especially schools, create problems for scholarly writing. They focused largely on the earliest phases of the scholarly career: school and just beyond. This chapter and the next look at writing problems as they arise at later stages of a career in sociology. Pamela Richards discusses the crucial transition from the early post-student days to being a grown-up professional in the next chapter. This most immodest chapter in an immodest book tells some stories from the many years I spent in the business and draws some analytic lessons from them.

First lesson: no one learns to write all at once. Learning goes on for a professional lifetime and comes from the variety of experiences academia makes available.

Sociologists don't think of writing as a serious problem until they have trouble getting their work written or published. They may dismiss it as blithely as an acquaintance who said, "Writing style? You mean when to use italics and put in footnotes?" They may treat the skill of writing as a gift of God they just didn't receive (like the student who explained to his thesis committee, of which I was a member, that he knew his thesis was badly written but "I'm not verbal"). They may realize that they have difficulty saying what they mean, but they think that they can farm the job out. The nonverbal student said it was OK because his wife was an English major and could take care of any problems. Others hope that hiring an editor they can ill afford will solve their problem.

Not everyone develops my sensitivity about writing clearly. I can pinpoint some of the events of academic life (largely lucky accidents I was, for whatever reason, ready to respond to) that sensitized me.

English courses had something to do with it. As an undergraduate at the University of Chicago, I took a good, practical course in writing, which concentrated on techniques of organization and rewriting. I probably learned there that the first draft was just a first draft that I should routinely expect to rewrite. On the other hand, a few years of graduate school, reading sociology books and journals, gave my style all the typical features I now edit out of my own writing and my students' work.

After I got my degree, several experiences with people who were now academic colleagues rather than teachers reminded me of that undergraduate wisdom. I got a PhD in sociology from the University of Chicago in 1951, at the age of twenty-three. No surprise, I had trouble finding an academic job. Why would anyone hire such a child when they could have a full-grown adult for the same price (at that time, four thousand dollars a year)? I was lucky to get a research job, studying marijuana use, at seventy-five dollars a week. During the Christmas vacation, a Chicago streetcar fell over onto an automobile driven by a member of the teaching staff of the Social Science II course in the University of Chicago College. They needed a replacement in a hurry, and some friends already teaching the course knew and vouched for me, so I got the job. That's how I met Mark Benney, a British journalist who had begun adult life as a petty criminal and ended up teaching social science through the encouragement and help of David Riesman and Everett Hughes. He had published several books, and his experience as a professional writer showed in the grace and clarity of his prose, which I admired. Small, thin, and prematurely bald, Mark had a devious way I attributed to his prison stretches. He was careful about what he said, so if he said something serious, you knew he meant it, and meant you to take it seriously.

I had already published an article or two in professional journals and must have thought I was pretty good, or at least competent. I drafted a paper based on my thesis, the study of Chicago public school teachers I've already mentioned. It raised some problems about education and social class that I thought would interest Mark, so I asked him to read it. When he gave it back, he said it was very interesting and then raised some points about the substance. Seemingly as an afterthought, he added, "Of course, I suppose you have to write it in that funny style to get it published in a sociological journal." I knew he was a "real writer," so the remark stung, and I was determined to go back and do it again, using some of the lessons about rewriting I had learned in college. I began to see that finishing a paper might not mean you were done with it.

Several years later Jim Carper and I wrote an article based on our study of the occupational identities of graduate students in several fields. We submitted it to the *American Journal of Sociology*, then edited by Everett Hughes, who had directed my thesis research and to whom I felt close and loyal. The manuscript came back, with a note from the managing editor, Helen McGill Hughes (Everett's wife and a sociologist as well as an experienced journalist), saying that I was to understand that Everett really loved me, that he had written his editorial comments at four in the morning, and that I shouldn't take their violence literally. The comments certainly took me aback. Among other things, he said that whole sentences and paragraphs sounded like they had been translated from German, word for word. I didn't read German (or any other language, despite passing a university exam in French to qualify for the PhD), but I knew that was bad. One memorable paragraph, given here in its entirety, quoted one of our most ponderous sentences and added this commentary: "Stink! Stink! Stink!" Mark's casual joke had sensitized me. Everett's letter strengthened my desire to write clear, understandable prose that sounded like it had been English all along.

The final step in my addiction to serious rewriting came when Blanche Geer joined Hughes and me in a study of medical students. She took writing very seriously and taught me about it through serious discussions over single words in the drafts we were doing. We had wonderful and interminable discussions, for instance, about the term "perspective," a word and idea central to the theoretical apparatus of our study. What verb we should use with it? Did people "hold" a perspective, or "have" one? Maybe they "used" a perspective. Each word's overtones were different, and distinguishable, once we focused on them. So the question was not which word was right, but what we wanted to say. We discovered problems through stylistic discussion, but we finally had to solve them theoretically.

Our conversations taught me that it really mattered how you said things and that you had a choice in the matter. They also taught me that rewriting was fun, a kind of word puzzle whose point was to find a really good economical way to say something clearly. My talks with Geer completed my conversion to taking writing seriously and were by far the most important of all these experiences, because they continued through our writing of a number of papers and books together.

The sociologists I had gone through graduate school with had habitually traded drafts of papers-in-progress with each other, and we had been pretty good about telling each other what needed doing next. I don't think I realized how this reading and commenting and being read and commented on among peers affected my professional development until I hired Lee Weiner as a research assistant a few years after I started teaching at Northwestern. I was away the summer he began work, and as the conscientious revolutionary he then was, Lee (who later became one of the Chicago Seven) read all my correspondence, although it was not part of his duties. When I returned in the fall, he told me excitedly how much he had learned by looking through the folders I kept on papers I had written, seeing what my friends had written on, and about, succeeding drafts, and how I had taken those comments into account in my next version. (This good educational result of his nosiness made me forgive his "trespassing.")

Several years out of graduate school then, I had built a pretty efficient writing routine around rewriting on the basis of friendly criticism of early drafts. I had learned to see rewriting as fun, something like doing crossword puzzles, rather than an embarrassing task whose necessity revealed my shortcomings. I learned that thinking about writing, experimenting with my own style, and tinkering with other's work were fun too.

Maybe thinking of writing as an enjoyable game immunized me against the anxieties other people describe, but my relative lack of writing anxiety also had sociological roots. I had grown up in a strong theoretical tradition which also had a strong organizational base. The so-called Chicago school of sociology developed at the University of Chicago in the 1920s, under the leadership of Robert E. Park. (The Chicago school has over the years generated a long and interesting bibliography of critical historical works, from Faris 1967, Carey 1975, and Bulmer 1984 to Fine 1995, Platt 1996, Abbott 1999, and Chapoulie 2001.) It had a coherent point of view, embodied in Park's writings and developed and carried on by a cohort of powerful thinkers and doers, most prominently Everett C. Hughes, Herbert Blumer, Louis Wirth, and Robert Redfield. It also had a long list of classic empirical monographs to its credit: *The Gold Coast and the Slum*, *The Taxi Dance Hall*, *The Gang* and, later, *French Canada in Transition* and others. I studied, along with a couple of hundred other post–World War II students, with the giants of the post-Park generation and grew up on that pile of monographs. We knew there were other ways of doing sociology, but few of us took them very seriously. Growing up in that tradition and setting gave me a theoretical arrogance, the comforting conviction that I had essentially learned all the general theory I would ever need to know from Hughes and Blumer, and that the theory was good enough to deal with any problem that came up. I knew, and know, better intellectually, but that hasn't affected the emotional result.

Knowing you are essentially right takes a lot of pressure off your writing, since you don't try to solve sociological problems by finding the just-right way to formulate them. Some people solve theoretical problems by logical analysis. I learned to decide theoretical problems empirically. Either way is better than trying to do it by finding the right way to say it.

The ever-growing number of sociologists and sociological specialties has produced a similar increase in sociological organizations and journals. (See, for example, Jacobs 2016.) Sociologists edit these journals, and editorial jobs are usually one of the unwanted tasks, because they involve so much work with so little reward (Abbott 1999, 165–92), honors that come to people who have been in the business for a while. Graduate training programs do not teach you how to edit a journal—how to edit papers, how to deal with the printer, how to coax authors to improve their work, or any of the other difficult jobs that come with the honor. Most journals cannot afford professional editors, so the sociologists who become editors do all that themselves. They learn the job by doing it, with the help of a few tips from their predecessors. My experiences as an editor, during which a hobby became a second profession, contributed a lot to my views on writing.

After years of editing the works of friends and colleagues informally, I took on two serious editorial jobs. In 1961 I became editor of *Social Problems*, the official journal of the Society for the Study of Social Problems, an organization that had been started in opposition to the monolith the American Sociological Association was turning into. I understood my job to be (and I think it was so understood by those members of the SSSP who had an opinion) to put out a journal that was somehow different from the "establishment" *American Sociological Review* and *Amer-*

ican Journal of Sociology. I wasn't sure what that entailed, but I thought I ought to try to find a home for articles that were not welcome, for one or another reason, in the larger journals.

What would make an article unwelcome? Most SSSP members thought that the "establishment" favored heavily quantitative work, work based on structural-functional theory, and work that was apolitical (and therefore in a real sense conservative). The SSSP thus favored work that was nonconservative, not biased toward the quantitative, and used either "Chicago" or, in later years, Marxist theories. In any event, it wanted to be open to whatever wasn't Eastern establishment. I must have accepted all that as reasonable, even though establishment journals had published my own nonquantitative, non-structural-functional work often enough.

So I took over as editor with the notion that my responsibilities consisted of publishing antiestablishment materials. I had also decided (though no one made this part of my official or unofficial responsibilities) that I was going to do something about what I thought was the sad state of sociological writing by rewriting what appeared in the journal as much as necessary. With that in mind, I recruited people for my editorial board who wrote well and knew what good writing was, people I could count on to help me.

I learned a lot from my first few issues. Once I assembled my first issue (and I'll speak about those problems shortly), I rewrote every paper in it extensively. That was a more intensive and more educational experience of editing than I had ever had. Doing so many papers by so many people in so many styles in such a short time made me feel like a newspaper copyeditor. I learned to go through a paper rapidly and to spot the things I knew I would without doubt change immediately. (I never understood how I did some of what I learned to do: for instance, to spot a typographical error in a page of galley proofs from across the room when I couldn't even read the type.) But I also learned that I was not going to rewrite all the papers that way, much as they might need it. It took too long, and I had other things to do. I might do a few pages of a piece, to show authors what I had in mind, but after that they would have to do it themselves or it wouldn't get done. No scholarly journals can afford what it would cost to edit journal articles the way, say, a money-making textbook is rewritten.

I learned another lesson when I assembled the articles for my first issue. A journal is supposed to come out regularly, every second month, like the *AJS* or *ASR*, or quarterly, like *Social Problems*. If you missed your deadline, you lost your turn in the printer's queue, people complained about their magazine being late, and the officers of the sponsoring organization wanted to know what was wrong. Better to come out on time. That did not mean that you published work you didn't think was good, but that you published work that was good, no matter what its breed: quantitative or qualitative, Chicago-style or structural-functional. Every journal editor I have ever talked to has agreed that, whatever prejudices they secretly expected to implement on assuming office, they soon found that the main thing was to get enough decent articles to fill the journal and get it out on time. Authors who think editorial prejudice accounts for their work being turned down or sent back to "revise and resubmit" are, for that reason, almost always wrong.

Of course, a lot of prejudice can be hidden in the definition of a "decent article." But here I am convinced by Stinchcombe (1978), who argues that when sociological analysts are doing good work they are all doing the same thing. Their work often looks more different than it is because they try to inflate its significance by using "portentous names," derived from "epochal theories" to describe what they do. (Many fields in the social sciences and humanities foster this practice, not just sociology.) Because good work is basically the same whatever its theoretical label, "good" is a professional and catholic judgment, like the judgments of musicians or dancers, who usually recognize when others are performing well, even if the judge doesn't care much for what they are doing. When sociologists show me work they think has been turned down because of prejudice, it is almost always badly organized and badly written. (I know that that is the voice of the establishment talking and don't know how to convince skeptics I'm right, other than to point to the contents of the journals which, during the period I'm speaking, of were always more various than critics thought.) The prejudices that do exist operate more subtly, as when the editor decides that one badly written, poorly organized piece is worth putting some special effort into, but not another. The lesson for people who do unpopular work is not that they can't get published but that they shouldn't expect editors to do their work for them. No one should, but some have a better chance of that happening.

I had a different editorial experience when I undertook to edit a series of books for the Aldine Publishing Company in 1962. Alexander Morin, then president and himself a social scientist, thought it would be worthwhile to put together a series that represented the Chicago tradition, broadly conceived. This led me to deal with book-length manuscripts and with authors who had the anxiety that goes with the commitment to a book. I also learned the necessity of thinking about how much a book could be expected to sell, not because Morin was a crass businessman but because if too many books lost money there wouldn't be any books or series at all. I learned the importance of subject matter and having something to say about it. People who did not care about your fabulous contribution to social theory might nevertheless read your book because they cared about the problems of death in hospital settings or the way mental illness was defined by family members, professionals, and the courts. We eventually published some fifteen books, and the series was reasonably successful, the sellers making up for the bad guesses.

Working as a book editor showed me a larger dimension of editing. I found that I could see an inner logic struggling to express itself in others' work more easily than I could see it in my own, just as I could see redundancy, fancy talk, and all the other faults in their prose more easily than in my mine. Since I wanted to criticize manuscripts in a way that would induce authors to fix them rather than just get mad (otherwise there would be no books for the series), I had to learn to be precise about what bothered me. I also had to tell them the facts of life about commercial publishing, that if books didn't sell the publisher eventually stopped trying to sell them.

My own experience with editorial prejudices has been minimal. The one area where I suffered a little had to do with a major change in the practice of sociology journal editors. My first articles, drawn from my master's thesis, were about jazz musicians. Following the practice of the exemplars I had used (e.g., Oswald Hall's articles on medical careers and Whyte's *Street Corner Society*), I quoted extensively from my field notes and interviews. But musicians didn't talk as politely as doctors (or as Hall reported they talked). They said "shit" and "fuck" a lot and, in the interest of scientific accuracy, and with a little mischief in my heart, I quoted them verbatim. That was acceptable in my thesis but editors in the fifties routinely replaced these words with dashes: "f——" and "s——." (This practice reached a height of foolishness in a postwar issue of the *AJS* devoted to the US Army, in which Fred Elkin's article "The Soldier's Language" ended up largely dashes.) I forget which of my articles was finally allowed to contain bad words written out; it might only have been when they were published in *Outsiders* in 1963. Of course, the forbidden words now appear routinely in sociology published in books and journals (and, in fact, in daily news stories).

When I described my writing seminar in chapter 1, I said that I had told the class about my own writing rituals, but I didn't say what they were. After I began giving the class, I started writing on a computer, which meant that I changed my routines over and over as computers and programs changed and made new routines possible. But here is what I told the class then; it's the way I wrote most of what I had written to that time. (What I can say of it is to be found in chapter 9.) The entire procedure was tailored to the rhythms of the academic year.

I was lazy, and still am, don't like working, and minimize the time I spend doing it. So, although I had written a fair amount, I spent relatively little time at a keyboard. I usually began what eventually became a paper by talking, to anyone who would listen, about the topic I was going to write about. When I began teaching, that meant talking to my classes about it. (*Art Worlds*, for instance, started out as the transcribed recordings of the lectures I gave the first time I taught the sociology of art, eight or nine years before the book was finished.) If I was invited to give a talk somewhere, I tried to persuade people that they wanted to hear about my "new research interest," that is, the paper I was beginning to work on. Those talks did some of the work of a rough draft. I learned what points I could get to logically follow one another, which ways of making a point people understood, and which ways caused confusion, what arguments were dead ends better not getting into at all.

I had not, when I began relying on talking as a way of getting something started, read David Antin's explanation of why he wrote by talking, but I recognized my own feelings in his description:

> *because ive never liked the idea of going into a closet to address myself over a typewriter what kind of talking is that? ive gotten into the habit of going to some particular place with something on my mind*
>
> *but no particular words in my mouth looking for a particular occasion to talk to particular people in a way i hope is valuable for all of us*
>
> (Antin 1976, i)

After talking about something for a while (usually several months or longer) I began to feel a restlessness I never recognized for the vague but real signal to start writing that it was. About the time I had to return from a summer vacation or an academic leave to my "day job" of teaching I would suddenly, with no premonitory symptoms other than this vague restlessness, sit down and start typing (this was in the old precomputer days) all day and half the night. I typed double-spaced on legal-size yellow ruled pads. I tore each sheet off the pad carefully (in all this showing my kinship with my students' similarly superstitious routines). If it didn't tear neatly at the perforations, I didn't use it. I didn't rewrite—not then, anyway—just kept typing. If I had trouble making a point or couldn't see how to end an argument, I typed brackets and wrote something like "I can't get anywhere with this now" and went on to some other point I could write about.

I added up my production frequently and announced to anyone I could persuade to listen that I had done six pages or, counting lines and estimating words to a line, 2,500 words. I tried to avoid crossing anything out, but was not rigid about it. If I saw a better way to say something, I replaced the old phrasing with something better. I also, quite neatly, inserted new passages where I thought them necessary, either by cutting and pasting or marking in the text on page 7 where the inserted material on my new page 7A would go. (It pleased me when secretaries complimented my neat manuscripts.) I sometimes wrote as many as three ten- to fifteen-page manuscripts—rough drafts of articles—in a three-week period.

I returned to my teaching job and spent the school year tinkering with these rough drafts. I often put them away for several months, seldom thinking about them as the routine of the university year—attending meetings, talking with students and colleagues—took over my daily life. That helped me rework the papers because, during the interim, I would forget why a particular point or way of expressing whatever-it-was had seemed so necessary and find it easier to change them. I might not take any of these folders out and begin rewriting until the Christmas vacation.

I always began by fixing sentences: cutting excess words, clarifying ambiguities, amplifying telegraphic thoughts. As I told my class, doing that invariably brought up the theoretical difficulties I had papered over, so that I soon had to reconsider my whole analysis. When I could, I wrote a new version of the parts that didn't work. If I couldn't, I didn't. In either case, I usually put the paper away again, for months or sometimes years.

When I began to write on a computer, things changed. Eventually I would make another draft. I could do this kind of work any time and usually spend no more than a few hours a day for three or four days at it. After a second or third draft, I had something I could send to some friends who might have helpful thoughts or harsh criticisms. I prefer hearing those criticisms in private from my friends rather than publicly in a "Letter to the Editor."

Some papers seem never to get finished, but I hate to waste anything I write and never give up hope, not even on pieces no one likes. Some things have sat around for many years, like the paper Steven Dedijer and I wrote on "Counter-Establishment R&D" in 1970, finally published in 2017. (In fact, I am still nursing an even older paper on the Abbey Theatre of Dublin that I wrote for Everett Hughes's class in ethnic relations in 1948.)

When I get criticisms and comments from friends, or from editors who have rejected a paper, I assume that I failed to make my points clearly enough to forestall those objections, and look for what I can do to meet the objections without changing my position (unless the criticism convinces me that the position requires changing). This revising and rethinking goes on until I can't think of anything else to do with it, or until some home for the piece presents itself (that is, until I am asked to prepare something for some occasion or volume, and what I've been working on fits the specifications). I've sometimes thought I was done with a piece of writing and then discovered I wasn't. How do I know that? When I see something that can be done better than it is, and see a way to do it, I know that I will have to go through the manuscript one more time. (I twice thought *Art Worlds* was finished before it really was.)

As I accumulated experience and became more cocksure, I began to set myself writing problems. Becoming dissatisfied with the long, complicated sentences I was writing, I started experimenting with short ones. How few words could I use? Very few. I also began searching for alternatives to the third person (too pompous) and the first person (tiresome in excess and often inappropriate). That led to an orgy of second persons, stage whispers to the reader: "You can see how this would lead to . . ."

Such a routine presupposes that the writer can afford to wait as long as I habitually do to finish things. When you write to a deadline—if, say, you have agreed to contribute a chapter to a book, and the deadline is approaching, or you have agreed to give a paper at the annual meeting of the American Sociological Association—you don't have that luxury. You don't have it, either, if you need publications to convince your colleagues or some administrator that you deserve promotion. One way around the latter problem is to do something that necessity forced on me early in my professional life. Because I had research, rather than teaching, jobs for many years, I always had to start new projects before I had finished old ones. As a result, I was always working on several generations of writing simultaneously: roughing out an initial draft of something new, rewriting initial drafts from an older project, making the final revisions in something ready for press. That is easier than it sounds. In fact, it makes every step of the process easier because when you get stuck on one job you can turn to another, always doing what comes easiest.

When I started making photographs in 1970, the standard photographic practices I then learned gave me more ideas about writing. I learned, as all photo students do, that the most important thing a photographer can do is photograph and that making thousands of bad photographs is no disgrace as long as you make a few good ones too and can tell the good from the bad. Students learn to "read" a contact sheet, made by printing a cut-up roll of film on one sheet of paper, so that each frame is reproduced at its actual size. You see every exposure you made, and you learn how to tell which one has an idea worth pursuing. It's the perfect way to learn that all that counts is the final product and that no one will criticize you for false starts and wrong ideas if you find something good in the process. I learned to be prodigal with film, paper, and my time. That carried over to my writing. I became more willing than ever to write down any damn thing that came into my head, knowing by analogy with photographing that I could always weed out what I didn't like or couldn't use.

Sometime in the seventies, I began to develop literary pretensions and ambitions. I think this started when a friend who was a "real writer" (a writer, that is, of fiction) said kind things about some drafts of an essay I was writing on art worlds. I began to wonder if I couldn't make the writing better in a more extended sense than just clarity. I began experimenting with a kind of organization I had barely been aware of before. I began to plant the seeds of ideas to be explored later in the early sections, and to introduce examples that I would later use to recall a complex point for readers. I quoted Anthony Trollope's story (from his autobiography) about relying on an old manservant to bring him coffee before he began writing and his comment that he thought that servant deserved as much credit as Trollope himself for the resulting books. I let that stand for the artist's dependence on the help of others for getting the work done, and later in the book I just referred to Trollope and his servant, expecting readers to recall the theoretical point.

Perhaps as a result of my experiences in teaching, I have become more and more convinced of the importance of stories—good examples—in the presentation of ideas. I used to be irritated when students told me that what they remembered from my sociology of art course was the story of Simon Rodia and the Watts Towers, which I told in enormous detail and illustrated with slides. I wanted them to remember the theories I was so slowly and painfully developing. Later I decided that the stories were more important than the theories. In a way, I should have known that, because I always began writing reports of field research by picking out representative incidents and quotes from my field notes and arranging them in some order, then writing a commentary on them.

Art Worlds also introduced me to the problems and opportunities of illustrations. It was obvious that a book on the arts should be illustrated. I first experimented with that possibility in a mischievous way. The *American Journal of Sociology* had accepted, after many revisions, an article called "Arts and Crafts," which addressed the way some craft media was taken up by worlds of art.

In the course of the paper, I described a number of artworks that illustrated my analytic points. When the article was accepted, I called the managing editor and asked if she didn't think some illustrations would be appropriate. The *AJS* almost never published pictures, other than portraits of deceased members of the University of Chicago Sociology Department, and I think I assumed that she would say no, and I could then feel discriminated against. Naturally, she said that she would ask the printer and the editor, but thought they would say yes, as they did. Now I had more work to do, finding pictures that really made the points I wanted to make and for which I could get prints at a reasonable cost. The text had referred to Robert Arneson's ceramic sculpture of a teapot whose spout was an erect penis, and to a photograph of a nude woman by Edward Weston. I thought that perhaps there would be trouble over these (the Weston photograph included pubic hair, which had only recently made *Playboy*) but my prejudices were wrong again.

When I put the book together, I knew that it would have pictures. Grant Barnes, my editor at the University of California Press, gave me a wonderful piece of advice. He said, "Don't put captions on the pictures that just identify them. Say at least a sentence explaining what the reader should see in the picture." Since I followed that advice, a reader can get the gist of the book just by looking at the pictures and reading the captions. All this has increased my interest in the visual aspects of writing and bookmaking.

To repeat the moral, you learn to write from the world around you, both from what it forces on you and from what it makes available. The institutions scholars work in push them in some directions, but also open up a lot of possibilities. That's where you make a difference. I have been relatively open to the possibilities, perhaps more than most, and resistant (again, perhaps more than most) to the pushes. The world does push and sometimes it hurts to resist. But my story, I think, for all its historical and personal peculiarities, shows that the opposite is truer than most people think.

6 : Risk   BY PAMELA RICHARDS

The bulk of this chapter was written by Pamela Richards, a sociologist who used to teach at the University of Florida, but it needs some introduction and explanation. I had been very pleased with the results of asking Rosanna Hertz to write to me about what she meant when she said that some ways of writing were "classy." I was therefore on the lookout for a chance to see what else I could discover by persuading people to write to me about what they meant by their offhand remarks. I didn't have long to wait.

I have known Pamela Richards since she began her graduate work at Northwestern. After graduating and beginning her teaching career at Florida, she continued to do technical statistical studies in criminology, in the style of her dissertation. After several years, she decided to try something different and use her substantial fieldwork skills to do a study of the Florida state women's prison located near Gainesville. She thought the study would be more difficult than it turned out to be. The prison officials made her entrance easy, and the residents, initially suspicious, soon talked to her freely and gave her access to most prison activities.

After a year she had accumulated a substantial file of field notes and knew a great deal about life in this prison. She thought she ought to begin writing up her results. We had corresponded earlier about her fieldwork problems, so she confided that she was having trouble getting started. Since she had successfully written up her earlier research, she thought there might be something about qualitative materials that required a different approach, and she asked me about it.

I brought out my standard remedy, mentioned earlier, suggesting that she sit down and write whatever came into her head, as though the study were done, but without consulting her field notes, the literature on prisons, or anything else. I told her to keep typing as fast as she could. When she got stuck, I suggested, she should type in "I'm stuck" and go on to another topic. Then she could read the results and see what she thought was true. In that way, she would find out how to analyze her field materials, because she would have to check them to see if what she thought was true really was and, if not, what was. In any case, I said, she could produce a lot of the rough draft quickly, and that would be a start.

I have given this advice to many people over the years. Not many take it. They don't argue with me, they just don't do it. I had always found that hard to understand, but the results of my advice to Pamela helped me to see why they were so balky. She wasn't balky, but, because she was reflective and articulate, she could make clear what others had found troublesome.

For a while, I heard nothing from her. Then she wrote to say that she had followed my advice and was enclosing the fifty pages she had written in ten days as a result. That tickled me, of course. It's rewarding to see your advice pay off. But her accompanying letter raised what turned out to be an important question, one for which, with a little prodding, she provided a wonderfully detailed answer.

She wrote that she had rented a cabin in the woods to live in while she tried the experiment of writing the draft. "Even though

I knew it would be a very high-risk operation," she said, "I decided to try it anyway." I couldn't understand what she meant. She was a well-established professional who had published in respected journals and coauthored a book. She gave papers at professional meetings and had just been promoted and given tenure. She had, in other words, been through the scariest trials that afflict young academics. Where was the risk?

Here was my chance to use the "research method" that had been so successful with Rosanna Hertz. I asked Pamela to explain what was so risky about sitting at a keyboard for ten days and writing any damn thing that came into her head. At worst, I pointed out, she would have wasted the time she had spent on it, but that can never be much of a price for someone who otherwise might not have written anything at all.

Again I didn't hear for a while. Then I got the letter that follows, explaining honestly and personally what lay behind that casual remark. I originally intended to use what she wrote as raw material for an analysis of the problems of risk. As I reread what she had written, however, it was clear that I had nothing to add to her story-and-analysis. So I asked her if she would be author of the body of this chapter, for which I would simply write an introduction and whatever else was necessary to relate it to the rest of the book. She agreed. It's an unorthodox way of doing things, but it seems the best and most honest way of getting what needs to be said said. What follows is her letter answering my question.

Dear Howie,

I just finished two cups of coffee while thinking about the issue of risk. My meditations have to start with three dreams that I've had in the last week. Two are about risk (among many other things, I'm sure) and one is about pushing through the risk. Actually, only two are dreams, the other is a different sort of midnight event that I suffered through right before I received your letter.

In my first dream, I had sent copies of three chapter drafts to a close friend I've known since graduate school. They were the same drafts that I'd sent to you. (In reality I haven't sent her anything yet.) She and I met at the American Sociological Association meetings in San Francisco, and she brought a huge stack of written comments with her. She was *angry* with me, and the comments were scathing. They went on for page after page: "This is absolutely the stupidest stuff you've ever written. . . . How could you say such things?. . . . Don't you realize the politically objectionable nature of what you've said here. . . . What's wrong with you, haven't you any sense at all? . . . This is nothing but bullshit. . . ." As I read through the stack of comments, she sat there and simply glowered at me, and I felt like she wanted to take me by the shoulders and shake me till my teeth fell out. Naturally I began to cry—silently, with the tears running down my face. I wanted to wail and keen and run away, but because we were at the meetings and there were all these *colleagues* around, I had to keep as good a face on it as possible. I felt terrible. Betrayed, perhaps, but mostly as if I had let her down. I felt that I had failed to measure up to what she expected of me, and that this preliminary work had somehow demonstrated that I was a shit—intellectually, personally, politically, and morally. I struggled up from the table where I was reading the comments. She leaned back in her chair and watched me. Her face was cold and the anger had turned to disgust. Then somehow I was pushing my way through a crowd of conventioning sociologists (none of whom I knew), trying to get out. I kept bumping into them, saying "Excuse me," but no one responded much. They didn't even really look in my direction when I ran right into them. Then I woke up.

Now for some balance. I had a second dream that night, it seemed to be right after that one. (I'd been reading Lillian Hellman's An *Unfinished Woman* and *Pentimento*. Over and over and over. I don't quite know why.) In the second dream I was sitting in a chair composing things for the book on the women's prison. I'm not sure what chapter or what topic, but the words were flowing beautifully. I wasn't writing them down; instead I was speaking them, and they just rolled out of my mouth. Everything was perfect, the style was gorgeous, and I was conscious of the fact that it all sounded as if Lillian Hellman were writing it—it was exactly the same style, the same marching sentences, the same feel and expression. It was wonderful. I felt very powerful and fully in command of what I was doing. I knew it was good stuff, knew it was elegant, and even began gesturing as I was speaking, almost as if it were oral interpretation. When I awoke, I just sort of floated up into consciousness slowly and comfortably, very pleased with myself and what I had accomplished.

But then, two nights ago I flashed out of a deep sleep (no dream this time) with a perfectly formed, crystalline conviction. I *knew*, absolutely and with complete certainty, that I was a fraud. The knowledge wasn't constructed through some explicit argument; it didn't develop out of anything I recognized; it was just there. So I began turning it over in my mind, trying to see what might be on the underside, and it began to take on better form: "I am a fraud because I don't work the way everyone else does. I don't read the classics as bedtime reading; hell, I don't read anything except weird novels and stuff that has nothing to do with my 'work.' I don't sit in the library taking notes; I don't read the journals cover to cover; and what's worse, I don't want to. I am not a scholar. I am not a sociologist because I don't know any sociology. I haven't the commitment to steep myself in the ideas and thoughts of The Masters. I couldn't converse meaningfully about The Literature on any topic including those in which I am allegedly a specialist. Even worse, I have the temerity to claim that I am doing a study of women's prisons, when in fact I haven't done it right. I don't know all sorts of things I ought to know, and can't seem to force myself to do it the way it ought to be done. Worse still, I know I have to go back soon and do another data push, filling in the holes, expanding things, and doing it right this time. And I don't want to. I'm too tired."

Not too useful for the middle of the night, right? God, it was torture. I went round and round on these sorts of things, getting angry and frightened by turns. I simply couldn't shake the conviction that I was a fraud. The main reason? I don't "do sociology" the way all my colleagues appear to do it, and the way it's supposed to be done. (And I've had a dry period as far as writing goes—almost two weeks—which leads rapidly to the conviction that I am a lazy parasite who doesn't do anything, anything at all.) The fact that I know that no one works the way they say they do, and that no one hews the perfect methodological line doesn't help much because I cannot translate this knowledge into gut-level belief. I feel vulnerable. Others can get me if I let on that I am a misshapen lump of a sociologist, even if they are equally misshapen.

So what does all this have to do with risk? For me, sitting down to write is risky because it means that I have to open myself to scrutiny. To do that requires that I trust myself, and it also means that I have to trust my colleagues. By far the more critical of these is the latter, because it is colleagues' responses that make it possible for me to trust myself. So I have dreams of self-doubt and personal attack by one of my closest and most trusted friends.

God, it's hard to trust colleagues. There's more at stake than simply being laughed at. Every piece of work can be used as evidence about what kind of a sociologist (and person) you are. Peers read your work and say, "Hell, that's not so bright. I could do better than that. She's not so hot after all." (And, by extension, they decide that your public act as a sociologist is fraudulent.) The discipline is set up in such a competitive fashion that we assuage our own insecurities by denigrating others, often publicly. There's always a nagging fear (for those of us who are junior, unknown sociologists) that even peers can make offhand comments about us that will become part of our professional image. If those comments are critical or negative, it's dangerous. This makes it very risky to give drafts of anything to peers. Few people understand what working drafts are. They assume that first drafts are just one step removed from being sent out for review. So if you show up with a working first draft, you worry about what could happen. They could decide that it's shoddy work, poorly constructed, and really quite sloppy. Their conclusion? That you're not much of a sociologist if you pass around such crap. And what if they tell that to others?

But say you can convince them that a working first draft is indeed a working draft, that it has been whapped out in a stream of consciousness fashion, that it is truly just for ideas. It's still terribly risky because the reader may not be looking for great grammar and well-turned phrases, but she is looking for stunning ideas. In some ways this is even more terrifying. It's ideas that are on the line, not ability to write. How often have you heard someone say, "Well, she may not be able to write, but god, is she brilliant!" It is OK to write like a college sophomore if you are bright. If you give someone a working draft to read, what you're asking them to do is pass judgment on your ability to think sociologically. You're asking them to decide whether you are smart or not and whether or not you are a real sociologist. If there are no flashes of insight, no riveting ideas, what will the reader conclude? That you're stupid. If she tells that to anyone else, it's the kiss of death. Hence the fear of letting anyone see working drafts. I cannot face the possibility of people thinking I'm stupid.

Most of these points also apply to letting sociologists other than your peers see your work, but with something of a twist. There are times when giving your work to senior colleagues seems even more dangerous than giving it to peers. Say you're an untenured faculty member. What is the practical outcome of getting known as a sloppy worker (scenario 1 above), or a concrete brain (scenario 2)? What if members of the tenured faculty reach this conclusion about you and your work? No grants, no job offers, no promotions. That's risky. Professional reputation is tied to professional position, and few of us have the power to say, "I don't care what you think."

To overcome these fears, to take the risk of being thought sloppy or stupid, you have to trust your colleagues. But the discipline is organized in a way that undermines that trust at every turn. Your peers are competing with you psychologically (ah, the perversity that allows me to feel better when someone else eats dirt) and structurally. Tenure, grants, goodies are becoming more and more part of a zero-sum game, as the academic world feels the current economic crunch.

So peers are hard to trust, especially those close to you: those in your department or those in your specialty. It's also very easy to fear your senior colleagues because you feel that they are constantly judging you. They're supposed to, because they are the ones who feel that they have the duty to weed out the good from the bad in this young crop of academics. They do talk to one another about your work and tell one another what they think of your potential. So how can you trust them not to tell tales when they decide that your work isn't very good?

This problem of trust is critical because it undermines the kind of emotional and intellectual freedom that we all need if we are to create. Who can you trust? I imagine there are a few people who are so confident that they don't really worry about what colleagues think, but they're a special breed, a very uncommon type. They just charge ahead, dropping off manuscripts left and right, filling up people's mailboxes with page after page of interesting and useful ideas. How is it possible? Some of them have the kind of personality that gives them this ability; others (most) have the structural freedom that gives them more power to say, "I don't give a damn what sociologists are 'supposed' to do, I'm doing what I want." I've noticed a little bit of this (a very little bit, I'm afraid) in myself now that I have tenure. It's not that I necessarily trust anyone more, it's just that I can be less concerned about the impact of their negative judgments.

But trust—. Who can you trust? When I think about the people I trust to read my work, I realize that they are people who already know how stupid I can be: the people I went to graduate school with, the people who taught me sociology while I was in graduate school, and a few people since that time whom I have come to know as friends as well as colleagues. People who knew me in graduate school have seen it all, and I know that with them there's only one way I can go: up. They've seen my early attempts to write and think, supported me through that, and believed that there was something lurking there beneath all the confusion. So I trust them. And, not incidentally, they trust me. We share things back and forth because of those early bonds. After all, nothing could rival the pain involved in those first attempts to sneak out into the world, scribble a few notes, and then come home and try to make something of it. And nothing can rival the exhilaration of having someone tell you that those tiny, tentative offerings were good. The colleagues since then who have also become friends are few but precious. Our mutual trust comes from having struggled to overcome the structural barriers that originally divided us. Like all friendships, they're the product of those cautious little dance steps that move you close together and then apart, near again and then farther away, each approach creating a bit more trust and concern. I have no prescription for creating those trusting friendships, though I wish I did. With me it's highly idiosyncratic, although it sometimes comes from working on a shared research project.

So these are the people I trust with working drafts. The professional risk is minimized by our common history. Their responses to me do something important, something absolutely critical if I am going to be able to continue to construct working drafts. Their responses convince me to trust myself, because for me, there's another great risk involved in writing. It's the risk of discovering that I am incapable of doing sociology and, by extension, that I am not a sociologist and therefore not the person I claim to be. The risk of being found out and judged by colleagues is bound up in the risk of being found out and judged by myself. The two are so closely interwoven that it is often hard for me to separate them. How can you know that you are doing OK, that you are a sociologist, unless someone tells you so? It's other people's responses that enable me to understand who I am.

These then are the twists of risk: I trust myself (and can therefore risk writing down my ideas—things that I have made up) primarily because others I trust have told me that I am OK. But no one can tell me that until I actually do something, until I actually write something down. So there I am, faced with a blank page, confronting the risk of discovering that I cannot do what I set out to do, and therefore am not the person I pretend to be. I haven't yet written anything, so no one can help me affirm my commitment and underscore my sense of who I am.

I need to mention something else about gathering confidence from the feedback of trusted friends. You have to trust these people not just to treat you right (not to be competitive with you, not to tell tales when you mess up), but also to tell you the truth. I must believe *absolutely* that if I write crap or think idiotic thoughts they will tell me. If I can't trust them to tell me the truth, then their feedback will not help me trust myself. I'll always wonder whether my ideas are really good, or whether they're just trying to be nice. The feeling that someone is humoring me is more damaging to my sense of self than outright attack. Sure, we all tell little white lies to each other. But there's got to be an underlying honesty, or I really start spinning. We must believe that it's no sin to make mistakes and no sin to criticize, otherwise feedback is useless.

How do I try to deal with all this risk and get myself moving? To begin writing at all, I sometimes have to look backward. I say to myself, "Well, I may not have written about prisons before, but I did write about juvenile delinquents, and people seem to think that was acceptable." It's at least a small bit of comfort. Or I look far to the future: I call trusted friends and tell them about my work. I run on and on, they make appropriately comforting noises, and then I feel a bit stronger. Sometimes I feel strong enough to begin writing. There's something that I think many of us believe: talking about work is less of a risk than writing about it. In part that's because no one remembers the ideas that you speak. But it's also as if we have an informal agreement not to hold one another responsible for anything we say. So I can throw out some safe comments, gather reinforcement, feel better about myself, and maybe take that first risk. But there is a catch here too. Because what we say doesn't count, it is easy to think of these conversations as inconsequential bull. But if I think that, then the listener's positive feedback is not credible, because I conclude she is responding to my act, my sociologist's facade, rather than to any meaningful ideas. If, however, I can learn to take talk seriously, people's responses can help me get the first words down on the page.

In some ways, writing gets easier the more you do it, because the more you do it, the more you learn that it's really not as risky as you fear. You have a history on which to draw for self confidence, you have a believable reputation among a wider number of people whom you can call on the phone, and best of all, you have demonstrated to yourself that taking the risk can be worth it. You took the risk, produced something, and *voila!* Proof that you are who you claim to be. Though I must also admit that it's not as easy as I'm making it sound. My writing history gives me some confidence, but I look at my past work with mixed emotions. It looks awkward and full of errors, and I tell myself that I must do better. My expectations change constantly, and I continually redefine what I consider to be good work. This means that every time I sit down to write I find myself wondering whether I can really do this stuff at all. So writing is still a risky activity.

But what I seem to be learning as I spend more time writing is that the risks are worth taking. Yes, I produce an appalling amount of crap, but most of the time I can tell it's crap before anyone else gets a chance to look at it. And occasionally I produce something that fits, something Lillian Hellman might have written, something that captures exactly what I want to say. Usually it's just a sentence or two, but the number of those sentences grows if I just keep plugging away. This small hoard of good stuff also helps me take risks. When I feel as if I simply cannot write, I sometimes go back and reread sections of something I've written that I like. It reminds me that there are two sides to risk. You can lose, but you can also win. I tend to think only of losing, and that makes me fearful. Rereading some good stuff can sometimes get me started when other stratagems fail. And I'm also seeing that the negative side of risk-taking isn't as bad as I fear. I can hide the worst of the writing I do. No one besides me need ever see it—and I throw it out as quickly as I can. What I show others are things that I think have some merit, and even the occasional paragraph that rolls beautifully off the platen. In other words, I have some degree of control over the risks involved in writing and letting others see what I have done. I am not completely at anyone's mercy, not even the mercy of my own impossible demands for perfection. I am allowed to throw things away.

So. But it's the complexity of risk, its dual nature, that allows me to dream of being attacked by a friend and of writing like Lillian Hellman, both in the same night. As I write more and more, I begin to understand that it's not all-or-nothing. If I actually write something down, I'm liable to win a bit and lose a bit. For a long time I worked under the burden of thinking that it was an all-or-nothing proposition. What got written had to be priceless literary pearls or unmitigated garbage. Not so. It's just a bunch of stuff, more or less sorted into an argument. Some of it's good, some of it isn't.

I have nothing to add to this analysis. Pamela Richards has explored in detail the organization of peers and superiors characteristic of the world of the young academic she knew and shown vividly how it affects one's willingness to take the chances that trying to be a professional intellectual confront you with. Having two personal stories in this book gives you a feel for what is peculiar to the person and what is generic in the situation and process. I don't know how typical these feelings are of other fields. I think they afflict most academics and intellectuals.

7 : Getting It Out the Door

Tracy Kidder's *The Soul of a New Machine*, an account of an engineering team creating a new minicomputer, taught me a useful expression: "getting it out the door." People in the computer industry commonly used it (and may still, for all I know) to refer to the final stage in the development of a new product. It takes a long time to create a new product: conceive the idea; translate the idea into plans for hardware and get the hardware built; simultaneously create a software operating system to control the hardware and the applications that will make the machine worth building; write the instructional materials that will teach people how to use it; and finally see the product shipped out to users.

The industry used this special expression to allude to the many things that can interfere with anything getting finished. Many projects never got out of the door. The hardware didn't work the way it was supposed to. Suppliers didn't deliver the components they'd promised to have ready. But new computers often didn't get out of the door because the engineers who worked on them didn't think they were ready for release. The engineers were often right. The industry resounded with cautionary tales of machines released before they were ready, bankrupting companies, ruining the image of an essentially good product, and the reputations and careers of the people associated with it.

A common, superficially correct explanation attributes these disasters to a chronic tension between marketing people and engineers. Marketing people need the machine now. The competition has one, and the company will lose its share of the market if it doesn't bring something similar out soon. But the engineers know that with just a little more time they can make a better machine: freer of bugs, simpler and cleaner, more elegant, more completely embodying the vision they began with. They know that other engineers, if no one else, will appreciate those refinements and admire their ingenuity. The marketing people don't care about the elegance and perfection that impresses the engineers' peers. They think engineers are impractical cuckoos who would just as soon bankrupt the company by pursuing perfectionist pipe dreams. The marketers' operating standard is that the machine should be "plenty good enough," able to do the job it was designed for well enough to satisfy users. The rare engineer who successfully straddles the two worlds and integrates their differing standards commands everyone's respect as someone who can "get it out the door."

The tension between making it better and getting it done appears wherever people have work to finish so that a product can be released: a computer, a dinner, a class assignment, an automobile, a book. We want to get it done and out to the people who will use it, eat it, read it. But no object ever fully embodies its maker's conception of what it could have been. Human frailty, your own and that of others, makes flaws and mistakes inevitable. You forget to put in the salt, overlook some important bug in your program, commit a logical fallacy, leave out an important variable, write a shamefully awkward sentence, ignore the relevant scholarly literature, misinterpret your data—every form of production has its list of common mistakes. But maybe, we think, if I just go over it one more time, I can catch those mistakes and devise even better solutions to the problems I set out to solve.

Getting it out the door is not the only thing people value. A lot of important work in a lot of fields has been done with little regard for whether it ever got out the door. Scholars and artists, especially, believe that if they wait long enough they may find a more comprehensive and logical way to say what they think. The same attitude finds an honored place in professional folklore and tradition. The American composer Charles Ives just didn't care, in the later stages of his composing career, whether anything ever got out the door. His reputation rests on works he never considered completed, although they were, in some sense, but not his, done. In fact, little of his music would have been played had not determined players bullied and wheedled until he reluctantly let them have the scores. Even then, he gave them little help deciphering the complexities and ambiguities of his scrawls.

Makers often want to delay getting the product out the door, even when (as in the world of scholarly publishing) the creator is also the marketing division and knows exactly why it must get out, and soon. Some authors' work leaves their desks only when someone steals it. A publisher I knew went to an author's house and, with the collusion of the author's wife, stole a manuscript the author thought still needed a little more work, especially on the footnotes. The author did not complain when the book came out.

For writers, getting it out the door occurs in several steps. Their work goes through the first door when they show it to a circle of trusted friends and colleagues for comments and suggestions. Further doors lead to course instructors, thesis advisers, journal referees, publishers' readers, and eventually to the great anonymous public who can read the work once it is publicly available. Some writers first get hung up while still students, failing to turn course papers in world on time and accumulating record numbers of "incompletes." Some let their trusted friends see work only when isolation makes them desperate, and then give them highly polished, heavily reworked materials. Others show friends early versions, but balk at submitting anything for publication, insisting that they need to reread a few of the great masters, run a few more tables, spend a little more time on their bibliography—whatever excuse their work makes plausible.

I like to get it out the door. I also like to rewrite and tinker with organization and wording, But I soon either put work aside as not ready to be written or get it into a form fit to go out the door. My temperament—impatient, eager for frequent rewards, curious about how others will respond to what I have said—pushes me that way. Growing up in the popular music business, where you play every night whether you feel like it or not, whether or not what you play is as good as it can be, probably reinforced that temperament. Most importantly, Everett Hughes taught me that intellectual life is a dialogue among people interested in the same topic. You can eavesdrop on the conversation and learn from it, but eventually you ought to add something yourself. For him, your research project wasn't done until you wrote it up and launched it into the conversation by publishing it. That view has obvious roots in the pragmatic philosophy of John Dewey and George Herbert Mead, both influential in sociological thought and practice. It's also heavily moralistic.

Students and colleagues who have worked with me know just how moralistic, stubborn, and irritating I can be about getting it out the door. Why don't they finish their theses? Where is that chapter they promised? You're almost done—*what's taking so long?* I know, when I get like that, that I'm overlooking something. Nothing is ever so simple, so either/or. So I look for the rest of the story. And there's always more.

I found the other side of the story, following the computer metaphor, by asking whether you could get the product out the door too soon. The question answers itself. Computer businesses had ruined themselves by ignoring the engineers' warnings. But it goes beyond that. James Joyce was in no hurry to get *Finnegan's Wake* out the door. Many masterpieces result from years of patient reworking by people who seemed not to care whether the damn thing ever got done. At an extreme, exemplified by Ives, producers stop caring whether they ever finish anything. Some masterpieces, to be sure, get done quickly, but the chance that a little more work might turn "good" into "great" ought to slow anyone down, at least a little. Working slowly, sacrificing present rewards to produce something really valuable, spending twenty years to produce one book (as John Rawls did with A *Theory of Justice* [1972])—it's an appealing image, even to someone as practical as me.

So "get it out" and "wait a while" both have a lot to recommend them. The conventional (and only sensible) solution to the problem is to see that you are choosing between competing goods and try to balance them. But that recognition doesn't help much. Where should we strike the balance? It's the same problem.

The case of Ives suggests an approach. How could he be a composer and yet never finish a composition? He did it by being a certain kind of composer: one whose music was not played. Music that hasn't been finished can't be played. Players can, of course, take your score away from you and finish it by fiat, as some of them did to Ives. But Ives didn't have to finish anything, because he had chosen not to participate in the standard forms of cooperative musical activity, the conversation, of the music business of his day. Not caring whether his music was played or not, he really didn't need to finish it.

More generally, you can decide when to let your work out the door by deciding what part you want to play in the world in which work like yours is done. Saying that doesn't merely translate an insoluble question into another language, leaving it equally intractable. The new wording at least makes you think about and take into account the organizational rewards and punishments of different strategies.

When I talked with graduate students who had stalled on a dissertation, or with academic friends who can't write their research up or put articles into publishable form, I should immediately have stopped moralizing and talked instead about social organization. If I didn't sit on the preacher in me firmly, however, our talks degenerated into unresolvable and irritating moralistic arguments. I began lecturing them not to be perfectionists, to settle for what's good enough for the rest of us. I told them I'd never written a masterpiece and didn't ever expect to. What made them different?

They didn't like that. Why should they have liked it? They often didn't recognize or accept the diagnosis, which might well have been wrong, and then got equally moralistic. Getting things done just to be getting them done didn't seem very principled. In fact, it smacked of careerism. Academicians often speculate that people who "publish a lot" do so for unsavory reasons.

To understand the argument I've just described, we need to drop the moralism and see the problem in relation to the social organization of academic life. C. Wright Mills' conception of the *vocabulary of motives* (1940) helps here. Every society or social group has a list of understandable and acceptable reasons for doing things. So we can explain that we took a particular job because we "needed the money," or "like working with people," or are "interested in that kind of stuff," or because "it has opportunities for advancement." Those are all understandable reasons for doing things in contemporary society. We may not do things for such reasons, or approve of anyone doing so, but we understand that others who do are neither crazy nor evil. In other societies, people might explain that they did something because their mother's brother said they had to, or because God told them to. Some friends would understand my deciding to take a new job because I'm an Aries and that's the way Aries people are. But I would have to be very careful who heard me say I did it because God told me to.

We don't use our society's list of acceptable explanations only to talk to other people. We also ask ourselves why we do things and look for reasonable explanations in the same list. If we can't find one, we may not do what we had in mind, or we may wonder about our sanity. Who does things for no good reason?

The vocabulary of motives common in academia explains frequent scholarly publishing in a variety of ways, many unflattering. People do it to "get ahead," "make a reputation," "get a raise" and, saddest of all, "to get tenure." Such reasons imply that the author settles for second best, accepts work that is "good enough" just to get the result out the door and collect the reward.

Scholars who do get things done in a "reasonable time" find that analysis self-serving, an excuse for not finishing. They explain that they write "to contribute to science," "to take part in the scholarly dialogue," or because "writing is fun." I talk that way. These reasons sound Pollyannaish, maybe a little unbelievable. (People who suffer when they write find the idea that writing is fun particularly preposterous.) Nevertheless, some writers do things for these reasons. If you think of scholarly activity as a big game, then writing something, getting into the dialogue, or making a contribution can all be at least as much fun as winning a computer game. If, however, you focus on getting things right, then this emphasis on production smells of compromise. The rhetoric sounds self-serving, even immoral.

Such a moral duel leads nowhere. It's more useful to talk about the consequences of different ways of writing. In fact, the organization of academic life evokes and rewards both sets of motives, makes both of them reasonable and necessary.

How is the world of scholarship organized, and what part does writing and publishing play in it? What part do you want to play in it, and how will the way you write and publish affect whether you can play the part you've chosen? Good questions, for which, not surprisingly, no solid answers exist. Not surprisingly, because academics are as unwilling as others to study the organization of their social world. They don't want their secrets exposed or their favorite myths revealed as fairy tales. They like to tell stories of their experiences and draw vast conclusions from them about what makes sociologists tick, what career strategies work (I've done both in this book) and, especially, how "rational" the governing of universities is, despite the surface appearance of chaos or (conversely) how irrational they are. Systematic investigation of students, careers, or universities would surely violate their convictions, and so no one thinks it worth doing or cooperating with. Research that helps administrators in their housekeeping tasks, of course, does get done—more about that in chapter 9—but makes more trouble than help for the authors I mean this book for.

So no body of research exists to settle these questions. Still, we can make some beginnings. Little of what I say will be controversial. Like so much other knowledge of how society works, people really knew it all along, but would rather not have to think about its implications and corollaries. One of the sociologist's jobs is to say such things out loud and make everyone think about them seriously.

Scholarly worlds embody a deep ambivalence, mirrored in the opposing attitudes of get-it-out versus take-your-time. On their practical side, worlds of scholarship are what Everett Hughes (1971, 52–64) called "going concerns," oriented toward getting work done. Less practically, they take the long view of history, looking toward the development, over years, even centuries, of a body of practice and knowledge. In the practical mode, they are in business right now and have to deal with all the immediate problems of any going concern. They may not have to produce a new machine or application in order to keep a share of the market (although the competition for student enrollments, academic reputation, and money is somewhat analogous). But they do give birth to and support formal associations, which have annual meetings and publish journals, which in turn require that people write papers for oral delivery and publication. Scholarly worlds provide the pool of labor which staffs university departments and teaches the courses they give. Scholarly worlds produce the textbooks and other materials from which those courses are taught. Their members give interviews to news organizations and testify to legislatures on divorce, crime, nuclear power, natural disasters, or whatever the discipline is supposed to know enough to talk about.

Most of these activities require that someone get some writing done, get some product out the door. The organization of scholarly disciplines doesn't require any particular person to do these jobs. If I don't write a definitive book on the subject, you will; if not you, someone else. If neither of us writes the book, we may suffer; but the field will not. We will not be promoted, but someone will eventually write it, if the material to write it from exists, and they will get promoted while we continue to teach the introductory course.

Nevertheless, those activities open the doors through which our scholarly writing can be moved out. Professionals orient themselves to the deadlines and constraints the disciplines create. Being practical people, they compromise. They won't, for instance, write in formats that are too short or too long for the standard media in which their work might appear. They can achieve a reputation, like that of the engineers who get computers out the door, for producing what's needed, in the form that's needed, on time. From this perspective, it's easy to dismiss problems of writing, as I'm told one professor does when he explains to his graduate students that all they have to do is copy the formats that appear in the *American Sociological Review*. If you use the major journals as exemplars (in one of the senses that Thomas Kuhn used that term) you will have problems only until you have mastered the form. From then on, writing should be as effortless as typing.

The scholarly world—this is the other side of the ambivalence—is also oriented toward the long run. In that mode, it does not need more of the same. It needs new ideas. But the old formats make it hard for a different idea to get a breath. Erving Goffman was both stubborn and good enough to make professional gatekeepers accept the pieces he wrote in totally "impractical" lengths: sixty-page essays, too long for journals and too short for a book. Most people do not produce such strikingly original work and do not have the personal force which made his quixotic enterprises successful. But people who "take forever" to finish what they write are not as crazy, lazy, or self-indulgent as people like me make them out to be. They have simply oriented themselves toward the long run, in which meeting ephemeral deadlines for the sessions of the Midwest Sociological Society is really trivial and not worth bothering about. That is not foolish.

For the discipline as a whole, this is undoubtedly a good thing. So long as some people do one thing and some do the other, the various activities through which the scholarly world does what we expect it to do—teach classes, put out journals, create new ideas—all get done. But individuals may suffer by virtue of which of the world's jobs they take on. If you take twenty years to write a book that then turns out not to be a major intellectual event, you will certainly suffer. But if enough people try, the scholarly world will benefit. If we make that choice, we're playing for big stakes in a risky game and we ought to recognize that.

A few somewhat questionable assumptions underlie these analyses: for instance, that taking more time is necessarily better than taking less time. After all, shouldn't thinking about a topic for a year produce better ideas and deeper understanding? Won't the extra time allow you to polish your prose so that it more accurately and elegantly expresses your improved thoughts? Of course these benefits will follow! The more time you invest, the greater your return.

Writers who balk at working quickly and getting the product out the door also think that masterpieces take a long time to do, while magazine writers get their work done quickly. Who wouldn't prefer to write a masterpiece as opposed to a magazine piece? It's a questionable comparison. Should we try to write great masterpieces, or would we be better off aiming for good, clear prose that says what needs to be said in a way that convinces? Does science need masterworks of prose? What chance does something written in the conventional style of the scholarly journals have of being a masterpiece? The pretentiousness of the ambition won't stand a close look. Besides, the authors of the great masterpieces of Victorian fiction—Dickens, Thackeray, Eliot, Trollope—wrote them under the conditions of pulp-magazine writing, as chapters of serials that might not even have been finished if the early numbers had not sold well.

Equating time spent and quality may in fact be empirically false. Painting teachers encourage students not to overpaint a picture, continuing to put paint on the canvas until an initially good idea is buried in a muddy mess. Writers can worry a piece to death, fussing over adjectives and word order until readers respond to the effort that went into the polishing more than to the thought the prose was supposed to convey. More work may not produce a better product. On the contrary, the more we think about it, the more we may introduce irrelevant considerations and inappropriate qualifications, insist on making connections that needn't be made—until we bury the thought in Byzantine ornamentation. "More is better" is no more true than "less is better." Yes, writing needs reworking and thought. But how much? We should look for the answer pragmatically, not by consulting our prejudices.

A related assumption, whose puritanical bases are obvious, is that you ought to work hard on your writing, and that you do that by putting in long hours. Even if you don't actually write, you should at least sit at your desk and try. Suffer, if you can't write. Such Calvinism might result from lower-school training, from teachers who insist that you look like you're working even if you don't get anything done, who don't want you to enjoy yourself doing something else when you should be working.

Classic descriptions of writing problems have often included touching accounts of a sheet of white paper that begs to be written on, while the author confronting it sits frozen with anxiety. Every word seems wrong. Not only do the words seem wrong, they also seem dangerous. I knew someone who wouldn't get out of his pajamas until the first page of an article he was working on seemed perfect to him. He often used as many as a hundred sheets of paper trying to get the first sentence right, and finally had to give up the practice when he found himself still in bedclothes at dinner time.

Another kind of anxiety that deserves exploration was mentioned in chapter 1. It still afflicts me. Scholars know that the subjects they write about involve so much that ought to be considered, so many connections between so many elements, so much of everything that it seems inconceivable that it can be given a rational order. But that's our business: to arrange ideas in so rational an order that another person can make sense of them. We have to deal with that problem on two levels. We have to arrange the ideas in a theory or narrative, describe the causes and conditions that lead to the effects we want to explain, and do it in a logically and empirically correct way. Logically correct means that we haven't committed any of the well-known fallacies of incorrect reasoning (Fischer 1970 describes historians committing all of these fallacies). Empirically correct means that the order we describe should be the order that things really have in nature, as best we know it. Finally, we want our prose to make the order we have constructed clear. We don't want imperfections in our prose to interfere with our readers' understanding.

These two jobs converge and cannot be separated. I shouldn't say that so blithely. It is probably possible to outline and construct an argument in some other language than verbal. Mathematics and graphics are two alternatives that allow precise statement, and someone might work out a theory in one of those ways and not be able to put it into words. In any event, getting ideas in logical order requires a keen eye for fallacious arguments. One can learn to spot such errors. It is more frightening to try to describe empirical order accurately. We know we can't describe everything. In fact, one aim of science and scholarship is exactly to reduce what has to be described to manageable proportions. But what to leave out? And where should we put what we leave in? The empirical world may be ordered, but not in any simple way that dictates which topics should be taken up first. That's why people stare at a blank screen and rewrite first sentences a hundred times. They want those mystical exercises to flush out the One Right Way of organizing all that stuff.

Well, what if you don't get it organized properly? We looked at that problem in chapter 3. But what if (which is much worse), knowing that any organization of reality you make will likely be incorrect in some way, you don't get it organized at all? That's the deepest cause of the anxiety that strikes writers when they start a new piece of writing. What if we can't, *just can't*, make order out of that chaos? I don't know about other people, but beginning a new paper used to give me anxiety's classical physical symptoms: dizziness, a sinking feeling in the pit of the stomach, a chill, maybe even a cold sweat. The dual possibilities, one as bad as the other, that the world has no real order or that, if it does, I can't find it, now or ever, are philosophically, almost religiously, frightening. The world may be a meaningless mess, but that's not a philosophical position I can live with easily. Not being able to figure out the first sentence makes that possibility palpable.

Do I have a cure for the disease I've described? Yes and no. A lot of other activities, especially sports, provoke paralyzing fears that keep people from getting started. The advice of experts in these areas is always the same. Relax and do *it!*. You cannot overcome the fear without doing the thing you are afraid of and finding out that it isn't as dangerous as you imagined. So the solution for writing something that will not fully, logically, and completely master the chaos is to write it anyway and discover that the world will not end when you do. You might be able to do that by tricking yourself into thinking that what you are writing is unimportant and makes no difference—a letter to an old friend, perhaps. I know how to trick myself, but I don't know how others can trick themselves. So here is where the advice stops. You can't start swimming until you get in the water.

8 : Terrorized by the Literature

Students (and other scholars/writers) often, as I said earlier, talk about "using" this or that theoretical approach—"I think I'll use Durkheim"—as though they had a free choice of theories. In fact, by the time they begin to write about their research, they have made many seemingly unimportant choices of details that have foreclosed their choice of a theoretical approach. They decided what questions to investigate. They picked a way of gathering information. They chose between a variety of minor technical and procedural alternatives: who to interview, how to code their data, when to stop, what statistical tests (if any) to use. As they made these choices from day to day, they increasingly committed themselves to one way of thinking rather than other possibilities, more or less firmly answering the theoretical questions they thought were still up for grabs.

But sociologists, and especially students, continue to fuss about choosing a theory for a practical reason. They have to—at least they think they do—deal with the "literature" on their topic. Scholars learn to fear "the literature" in graduate school. I remember Professor Louis Wirth, one of the distinguished members of the so-called Chicago school, putting Erving Goffman, then a fellow graduate student of mine, in his place with the literature gambit. It was just what we all feared. Believing Wirth had not given sufficiently serious attention to some influential ideas about operationalism, Goffman challenged him in class with quotations from Percy Bridgeman's authoritative book on the subject. Wirth smiled and asked, sadistically, "Which edition is that, Mr. Goffman?" Maybe there was an important difference between editions, though none of us believed that. We thought, instead, that we'd better be careful about the literature or They Could Get You. "They" included not only teachers but peers, who might welcome an opportunity to show how well they knew the literature at your expense.

Students learn that they "must" say something about all the people who have discussed "their" problem before them. No one wants to discover that their carefully nurtured idea was in print before they thought of it (maybe before they were born) and in a place they should have looked. (Or did look and then forgot. Wirth also told us that originality was the product of a faulty memory.) Students want to show the world, and all the critics who may be out there laying for them, that they have looked and, believe me, no one has had this idea before.

A good way to prove your originality is to attach your idea to a tradition in which people have already explored the literature. Hitching your work to a well-explored scholarly star helps you to assure yourself that your work doesn't redo something already done. If you "use" Weber or Durkheim or Marx or Mead, the exegetes have preceded you, laying out the terrain, specifying what the questions *really* are, defining what work by who will be relevant to consider—and in general providing a surefire way of dealing with the literature: "See Chaim Yankel's exhaustive review (1993) of the literature in this area." This protective ritual effectively covers the author's ass, but works less well to produce good or interesting scholarship. The reasons, interesting in themselves, also illuminate the institutional bases of creativity and banality.

Writers should, of course, use relevant literature appropriately. Stinchcombe (1982) has pointed out six such major uses. (I intend my summary of his paper to exemplify what I will describe later as a good use of the literature, to provide an already thought-through piece of an argument you need.) Although Stinchcombe writes about the narrower category of "classics," what he has to say also speaks to our problem of "the literature."

Two of the six uses he discusses relate to early phases of research and are less relevant to problems of writing. As a source of fundamental ideas, the classics are very important at the beginning of a project; but by the time you start writing, you ought to have your fundamental ideas clear. Clear or not, you already have them and they have informed your work and done their best or worst. The classics' second function, as "underexploited normal science," as a source of empirical hypotheses, hunches, and hints, is similarly crucial in the prewriting stages. Stinchcombe also mentions an organizational function of the classics: to symbolize solidarity among people in a field. "It is the fact that we have all read these classics, or at least answered preliminary examination questions on them, that binds us together into an intellectual community." He worries about this function, thinking that it leads us to admire work that time may have shown to be wrong (as, he says, Whitney Pope showed that Durkheim was wrong about suicide): "What is destructive about admiration of the classics, then, is the halo effect, the belief that because a book or article is useful for one purpose, it must have all the virtues."

Three other important uses of the classics have directly to do with getting our writing done. A classic work of scholarship serves as a touchstone: "a concrete example of the virtues scientific work might have, in a combination that shows what work should look like in order to contribute to the discipline." As Stinchcombe says, this is what Thomas Kuhn meant when he used the term *paradigm* in the sense of an exemplar. The virtues Stinchcombe is talking about are not the ones you might expect:

First class science functions with aesthetic standards as well as with logical and empirical standards. These standards are not defensible by the positivist or the Marxist or the symbolic interactionist philosophies of science. . . . If we embed the examples of excellence in our minds, as concrete manifestations of aesthetic principles we want to respect in our own work, and use them as touchstones to filter out that part we throw away and that part we keep, we may very well manage to work at a level higher than we can teach. For we work by the standards embedded in the touchstone, standards we cannot formulate but can perceive if we use a paired comparison—is this piece as good as Simmel?

Stinchcombe here describes what I meant when I described editing by ear. If he is right, and these aesthetic standards can't be justified "scientifically," it follows that there is no sense trying to find the One Right Way to write what you have to say. Copying well-done work (especially its organization or format), however, is a wonderful way to find possible right ways.

Classics also serve as "developmental tasks for novices," showing them how much more complicated things are than they thought and bringing them up to the level of sophistication common in their field. This function is usually what people have in mind when they talk about the benefits of studying for qualifying exams. It probably contributes to the irrational way people think about the literature, and to the mindlessly ritualistic literature reviews that decorate so much scholarly work.

Stinchcombe calls a final use of the classics "intellectual small change." You cite Weber or Durkheim or Yankel (just as you use the catchwords of a school) to show what camp you belong to. To do this, you must use well-known names:

Imagine if our badges for the convention [he is referring to the annual meeting of the American Sociological Association] had our names, our institutions, and our favorite classic writer. So mine might read "Stinchcombe, University of Arizona, Max Weber." Suppose now, in a fit of preciousness, I write instead "Stinchcombe, University of Arizona, Paul Veyne." He is right now the person I am most intellectually excited about, and embodies the same virtues as Max Weber. But 90-odd per cent of the people I met would not know who I was talking about, so would not learn anything about the set of prejudices and intuitions to which I was declaring my loyalty. . . . [But] the use of classics as identifying badges tends to produce sects rather than open intellectual communities. The badges tend to become boundaries rather than guides.

Conventional reviews of the literature provide evidence of the author's allegiances in this way, but authors would be briefer and less obsessive if that were their main purpose.

The classics are not the same as "the literature." Sociologists worry about the classics, but they also worry about the literature of commentary and methodological discussion, about research reporting specific findings on the topic and discussions of those findings, all of which they feel responsible for (much as students know when they are "responsible" for material on a test).

None of these are intrinsically bad ways to use the literature, but none of them answers the question of how to use the literature on your research topic.

Science and humanistic scholarship are, in fact as well as in theory, cumulative enterprises. None of us invent it all from scratch when we sit down to write. We depend on our predecessors. We couldn't do our work if we didn't use their methods, results, and ideas. Few people would be interested in our results if we didn't indicate some relationship between them and what others have said and done before us. Kuhn (1962) spoke of this mutual dependence and cumulation as "normal science." Many sociologists use "normal science" pejoratively, as though it meant "*merely* normal science," as though all of us could expect to produce scientific revolutions every day. That's a total misreading of Kuhn, and foolishness as well. Individual scientists don't make scientific revolutions. Those revolutions take a long time. Large numbers of people, working together, develop a new way of formulating and investigating the problems they are interested in, a way which finds a home in lasting institutions of scientific work. To imagine that your report of your project will accomplish what takes all that time and all those people is wrong-headed. It's alright to aim for the stars, but we ought to have a decent regard for what is humanly possible. If making a scientific or scholarly revolution singlehandedly is our chief goal, we are bound to fail. Better to pursue the goals of normal science: to do a piece of good work others can use, and thus increase knowledge and understanding. Since we can attain those things in our own research and writing, we don't set ourselves up for failure by aiming at the impossible.

A scholar can try to work in isolation from others and without their help, like so-called naive artists who produce paintings and constructions without reference to any of the traditions or admired works of the medium they work in. Artists who do that usually produce exceptionally eccentric work, but their work is also free of the constraints imposed by standard ways of working. That freedom from organizational constraint sometimes allows naive artists to produce works which command the respect of an established art world and which may even eventually be absorbed into its tradition (see the discussion in Becker 1982a, 236–48, 258–69). The dialectic of constraint and opportunity that naive artists illustrate affects all of us as we write our dissertations, papers, and books. That dialectic suggests two questions: how can we use the literature effectively? How does the literature get in our way and prevent us from doing our best work?

Are there effective ways to use the literature? Of course. For one thing, scholars must say something new while connecting what they say to what's already been said, and they have to do it in a way whose point readers will understand. They must say something at least minimally new. Although the empirical sciences pay lip service to the idea of replicating results, they don't pay off for it. At the same time, as you approach total originality, you interest fewer and fewer people. Everyone is interested in the topics people have studied and written about for years, both because the topics are of great and continuing general concern (why do people commit suicide?) and because they have been studied for so long that they have created the kind of scientific puzzles Kuhn (1962) identified with normal science (the literature investigating Durkheim's theory of suicide exemplifies this). The ideal scholarly contribution makes readers say: "That's interesting!" As Michael Schudson suggested to me, students must learn to connect their work to the literature in just that way, to set their results in the context of accepted theories that make it unlikely.

I remarked earlier that my use of Stinchcombe's article exemplifies what I think is a better way to use what others have done. Here's what I meant. Imagine that you're doing a woodworking project, perhaps making a table. You have designed it and cut out some of the parts. Fortunately, you needn't make all the parts yourself. Some are standard sizes and shapes—lengths of two by four, for instance—available at any lumberyard. Some have already been designed and made by other people—drawer pulls and turned legs. All you have to do is fit them into the places you left for them, knowing that they were available. That's the best way to use the literature. You want to make an argument, instead of a table. You have created some of the argument yourself, perhaps on the basis of new data or information you have collected. But you needn't invent the whole thing. Other people have worked on your problem or problems related to it and have made some of the pieces you need. You just have to fit them in where they belong. Like the woodworker, you leave space, when you make your portion of the argument, for the other parts you know you can get. You do that, that is, if you know that they are there to use. And that's one good reason to know the literature: so that you will know what pieces are available and not waste time doing what has already been done.

Here's an example. When I was working on the theory of deviance (eventually published in *Outsiders* [2018]), I wanted to argue that when others labeled someone as a deviant, that identification often became the most important thing about the person so labeled. I could have worked out a theory about how that happened, but I didn't have to. Everett Hughes (1971, 141–50) had already developed a theory describing the way statuses develop a halo of "auxiliary status characteristics," so that readers of that (very different) time would have expected an American Catholic priest to be "Irish, athletic, and a good sort who with difficulty refrains from profanity in the presence of evil and who may punch someone in the nose if the work of the Lord demands it." Or, to take a more serious example, although all you need in order to practice medicine is a license from the state, people in that era commonly expected doctors to be white male Protestants of old American stock. Hughes was especially interested in the intersection of race and professional position and, in developing his argument, made the following observation:

> Membership in the Negro race, as defined in American mores or law, may be called a *master status-determining trait*. It tends to overpower, in most crucial situations, any other characteristics which might run counter to it. But professional standing is also a powerful characteristic—most so in the specific relationships of professional practice, less so in the general intercourse of people. (147, emphasis added)

The idea of a master status-determining trait, which takes precedence in identifying people socially, was no more than an aside in Hughes's article. If I were to write an article titled "The Sociological Thought of Everett C. Hughes" in 2019 I would not spend much time on it and would no doubt make much of the historical changes in these matters. But, in working out my theory, I wanted precisely to talk about how a disreputable status characteristic like being addicted to drugs could spoil reputable statuses—genius or priest or doctor or whatever—one might think would neutralize it. Hughes wanted to talk about how the status of Negro at that time overpowered the status of doctor. I wanted to talk about how the status of junkie overpowered the status of son or husband, so that parents or spouses locked up the family silver and jewels when their beloved dope-fiend relative came to dinner. I wanted to talk about what a character in Doris Lessing's novel *The Four-Gated City* meant when she said that she didn't mind being thought schizophrenic but didn't like people to think that that was *all* she was.

Hughes's language fits my case exactly. I didn't need to invent the concept; he had invented it for me. I only had to bring it up-to-date. So, instead of creating yet another unnecessary new sociological term, I quoted Hughes and went on to make more use of his idea than he had in the article I took it from. In the same way, I had no need to work out the uses of the classics. Stinchcombe had done it. I only had to quote and summarize.

Is working that way plagiarizing or being unoriginal? I don't think so, although fear of such labels pushes people to desperate attempts to think up new concepts. If I need the idea for the table I'm building, I'll take it. It's still my table, even though some parts were prefabricated.

In fact, I am so accustomed to working this way that I am always collecting such prefabricated parts for use in future arguments. Much of my reading is governed by a search for these useful modules. Sometimes I know I need a particular theoretical part and even have a good idea of where to find it (often thanks to my graduate training in theory, to say a good word for what I so often feel like maligning). When I wrote my dissertation about Chicago public school teachers, I found modules I needed in the writings of such classic sociologists as Georg Simmel and Max Weber. Discussing how teachers expected school principals to take their side in any argument with a student, whatever the facts of the case, I found a general description of the class that phenomenon belonged to in Simmel's essay on superiority and subordination: "The position of the subordinate in regard to his superordinate is favorable if the latter, in his turn, is subordinate to a still higher authority in which the former finds support" (Simmel 1950, 235). I also wanted to argue that the desire of school personnel to keep parents and the general public out of school affairs was a specific instance of a phenomenon important in organizations of all kinds. I found that module in Max Weber: "Bureaucratic administration always tends to be an administration of 'secret sessions'; in so far as it can, it hides its knowledge and action from criticism. . . . [T]he tendency toward secrecy in certain administrative fields follows their material nature: everywhere that the power interests of the dominant structure toward the *outside* are at stake . . . we find secrecy" (Gerth and Mills 1946, 233).

On the other hand, I didn't know I needed the next module until I found it; then I couldn't do without it. It did not come from one of the conventionally recognized classics, although the work it is in is elegantly excellent. Willard Waller helped me and my readers understand why schools had a discipline problem when he said: "Teacher and pupil confront each other in the school with an original conflict of desires, and however much that conflict may be reduced in amount, or however much it may be hidden, it still remains" (Waller 1932, 197).

I also collect modules I have no present use for, when my intuition tells me I will eventually find the use. Here are some ideas I stored away from time to time, expecting eventually to find a place for them in my thinking and writing: Raymonde Moulin's (1967) idea that, in artworks, economic and aesthetic value are so closely related as to be the same thing, and Bruno Latour's (1983, 1984) idea that scientific inventions create new political forces, as Pasteur's work in microbiology did by introducing the microbe as a social and political actor. I may not use these ideas in their original form. I may transform them in ways their inventors wouldn't recognize or approve of, and interpret them in ways students of these thinkers will find incorrect. I will probably use them in contexts quite different from those they were first proposed in, and fail to give due weight to theoretical exegeses which strive to discover the core meanings their inventors intended. But I carry them with me, ready to apply when I make my observations or begin writing. It will be easier to use them, of course, if I have had them in mind all along. But I may also find that I had some such idea in mind, only not very clearly, and that Latour or Moulin or Waller has done the hard work of clarification for me. I am grateful, recognize that as part of the cooperative work of scholarship, and cite and quote them in the appropriate places. My work may look like a patchwork quilt as a result. When that happens I console myself with the example of Walter Benjamin, the German-Jewish man of letters, whose methods Hannah Arendt described this way:

> From the Goethe essay on, quotations are at the center of every work of Benjamin's. This very fact distinguishes his writings from scholarly works of all kinds in which it is the function of quotations to verify and document opinions, wherefore they can safely be relegated to the Notes. . . . The main work [for Benjamin] consisted in tearing fragments out of their context and arranging them afresh in such a way that they illustrated one another and were able to prove their *raison d'etre* in a free-floating state, as it were. It definitely was a sort of surrealistic montage. (Arendt 1969, 47)

That's the good side of the literature. The bad side is that paying too much attention to it can deform the argument you want to make. Suppose there is a *real* literature on your subject, the result of years of normal science or what, by extension, we could call normal scholarship. Everyone who works on the topic agrees on the kinds of questions to ask and the kinds of answers they will accept. If you want to write about the topic, or even use that subject matter as the material for a new topic, you will probably have to deal with the old way even though you think it quite foreign to your interests. If you take the old way too seriously, you can deform the argument you want to make, bend it out of shape in order to make it fit into the dominant approach.

What I mean by bending your argument out of shape is this. What you want to say has a distinctive logic that flows from the chain of choices you made as you did the work. If the logic of your argument is the same as the logic of the dominant approach to the topic, you have no problem. But suppose it isn't. What you want to say starts from different premises, addresses different questions, recognizes a different kind of answer as appropriate. When you try to confront the dominant approach to this material, you start to translate your argument into its terms. Your argument will not make the kind of sense it made in its own terms; it will sound weak and disjointed and will appear ad hoc. It can't look its best playing an opponent's game. And that phrasing puts the point badly, because what's involved is not a contest between approaches, after all, but a search for a good way to understand the world. The understanding you're trying to convey will lose its coherence put in terms that grow out of a different understanding.

If, on the other hand, you translate the dominant argument into your terms, you will not give it a fair shake, for much the same reasons. When you translate from one way of analyzing a problem into another, there is a good chance that the approaches are, as Kuhn (1962) suggested, incommensurable. Insofar as they address different questions, the approaches have very little to do with one another. There is nothing to translate. They're just not talking about the same things.

The literature has the advantage of what is sometimes called ideological hegemony over you. If its authors own the territory, their approach to it seems as natural and reasonable as your new and different approach seems strange and unreasonable. Their ideology controls how readers think about the topic. As a result, you have to explain why you haven't asked those questions and gotten those answers. Proponents of the dominant argument don't have to explain their failure to look at things your way.

My work in deviance taught me this lesson the hard way. When I began studying marijuana use in 1951, the ideologically dominant question, the only question "anyone" thought worth looking at, was "Why do people do a weird thing like that?" and the ideologically preferred way of answering it was to find a psychological trait or social attribute which differentiated people who did it from people who didn't. The underlying premise was that "normal" people, who did not possess the distinguishing causal stigma you hoped to discover, wouldn't do anything so bizarre. I started from a different premise: that "normal" people would do almost anything you could think of if the circumstances were right. Which meant you had to ask what situations and processes led people to change their minds about this activity and do what they formerly wouldn't have done.

The two ways of investigating marijuana use are not totally divergent. They can be made to coincide, and that's what I did when I first published this material in 1953: I made them coincide. I showed that users went through a process of redefining the drug experience that led them to regard it differently. Sociologists, psychologists, and others interested in drug use found that an interesting answer. It helped start a spate of studies of how people became this or that kind of deviant, mostly based on the premise that these were normal people who had just had some different experiences. Well, you might ask, what's wrong with that strategy?

What's wrong with it, something I did not realize until years later, is that my eagerness to show that this literature (dominated by psychiatrists and criminologists) was wrong led me to ignore what my research was really about. I had blundered on to, and then proceeded to ignore, a much larger and more interesting question: how do people learn to define their own internal experiences? That question leads to the exploration of how people define all sorts of internal states, and not just drug experiences. How do people know when they are hungry? That question eventually became of great interest to scientists who studied obesity. How do people know when they are short of breath or have normal bowel movements or any of the other things doctors ask about when they take a medical history? Those questions interest medical sociologists. How do people know when they are "crazy"? I think, looking back, that my study would have made a more profound contribution had I had oriented it to those questions. But the ideological hegemony of the established way of studying drugs beat me.

I don't know how people can tell when they are letting the literature deform their argument. It's the classic dilemma of being trapped in the categories of your time and place. What you can do is recognize the dominant ideology (as I did at the time with respect to drug use), look for its ideological component, and try to find a more neutral scientific stance toward the problem. You know you are on the right track when people tell you you're on the wrong track.

That goes too far. Of course. Is everything that disagrees with the dominant approach therefore right? No. But a serious scholar ought routinely to inspect competing ways of talking about the same subject matter. The feeling that you can't say what you mean in the language you're using will warn you that the literature is crowding you. It may take a long time to find out that this has happened to you, if you find out at all. I only saw my mistake about the marijuana study years later when I extended the argument far beyond where I had originally stopped (see the discussion in Becker 2014, 61–93). Use the literature, don't let it use you.

9 : Writing with Computers, Then and Now

THE BEGINNINGS

Computers—giant mainframe machines that universities installed for their own purposes—first appeared on university campuses (to my knowledge) in the early 1950s. In 1952, the University of Illinois, a pioneer, installed one of the first, ILLIAC, and soon made it available to researchers whose work required such then-massive computing resources. By sheer coincidence, I was a postdoc there at the time, connected to the psychology department, and heard about this New Thing early, because the Illinois psychologist Raymond Cattell, one of ILLIAC's pioneer users, needed that kind of computing power to calculate the large number of correlation coefficients (between the dozens of items in standard personality tests) as input for statistical techniques like factor analysis. Hardly anyone else had such needs at first, and sociologists weren't among those who did.

But relatively soon sociologists started to use lengthy survey instruments (made up of many dozens of "items"), administered to large numbers of respondents, to study all sorts of problems, and that led them to an increasing dependence on just such large-scale computing. By the time I arrived at Northwestern University in 1965, some of my colleagues spent a lot of time walking their data over to the computing center a few blocks away and then, a day or two later, picking up the tables the center produced for them. They knew relatively little about the machines and programs that turned their filled-out questionnaires into those tables.

And then Microsoft introduced Windows, the first computer interface designed for non-experts, and the individual PC (personal computer) that embodied it. That machine soon had a competitor, an upstart called the Apple II. Once again I was, by coincidence, in the right place for a box seat on an important development. Apple had started a program to sell their computers to professors and students through rebates to universities. This price competition faced resistance from the staffs of university computing centers, who worked on mainframes that ran on Microsoft software and used their reputations as experts on computing to fight this development. At Northwestern, that source of pressure was countered by my sociology colleague Andrew Gordon who, having worked on mainframes when he was in graduate school, thought the Apple II was a lot easier for non-statisticians (like me, for instance) to learn to use.

Raymond Mack, a jazz drummer I'd known in other connections, had been chair of the NU sociology department and in that capacity had personally hired both me and Gordon, and we were all good friends. Andy alerted Ray, now provost of the university, to the Apple program and to the institutional enmity of the computing staff to any competition to IBM. Ray took that seriously and Northwestern became one of the early participants in the Apple program. And I became one of the first Northwestern participants in it.

Guessing correctly that I'd be a good student, Andy gave me

personal lessons and held my hand through those tough first days of learning to be a computer user. He even gave me some lessons in elementary programming. As a result of which I finally proudly produced a program that did something sociological: opened a file for a Chicago census tract and used the population data it contained to draw a standard data display device called a population pyramid, a diagram made of two bar charts—one for males, one for females, for five-year age groups, the length of the bars indicating the number of people in that age/sex group in that geographic unit.

That, of course, was a sideline because I didn't, in my own sociological work, produce the kind of data that needed even that simple display of numerical data. But my new machine also let me type on it, and so I could record field notes (and that *was* the kind of data my research did produce), as well as endless other typed documents: analyses, explanation, and, finally, texts of journal articles and book chapters. I was as happy as a pig in mud!

CHANGES IN ROUTINE TASKS
No one doing scholarly work today can even begin to imagine the time everyone used to spend on the routine chores of an academic day. Nor how that compares with the now familiar experience of working with a computer. It might be helpful to be reminded of the time computers freed by releasing us from such repetitive, not very creative tasks, as typing.

When personal computers first appeared in our offices only a few of us took advantage of their possibilities. These unfamiliar looking machines looked something like typewriters. But their differences from those familiar machines seemed a little frightening, and most people at first thought they would mainly be useful for more sophisticated tasks involving numbers. Nevertheless, personal computers gradually began to catch on. More and more of us had them on our desks.

I was a relatively "early adopter," surprisingly for someone who didn't work with numbers much, and I became something of a model for others ("If Becker can do it, goddamn it, I can do it!"). A few adventurous quantitative sociologists had learned to work with a computer in the course of manipulating large bodies of numerical data, but hardly anyone who did fieldwork, interviewing, or historical research, all thought of as essentially language-based activities, had taken up this tool, so identified with "statistical" styles of work. The obstacles to following my lead were epitomized by a senior colleague who, looking over my shoulder as I worked, saw me delete a word and replace it with a better one, what many of us had already learned to call "cut and paste," since these new techniques had replaced the literal cutting and pasting (more accurately, "scotch-taping") involved in revising typed manuscripts., "How did you do that?" she asked suspiciously. When I explained and demonstrated the "cut and paste" commands, she wanted to know how I'd learned to do that. I said I'd read the manual. She wasn't sure she could do that, but I guided her through the steps and she became an enthusiastic convert. Universities provided instruction in these new skills, but a lot of people learned in this informal way.

I wrote the chapter about computers for this book's original edition in the first flush of my new enthusiasm, and of course it now sounds strange, even quaint, to readers who grew up with these machines the way my generation did with typewriters. But it's worth reminding ourselves of how computers relieved of us routine work that filled our time with tasks for which we now know simpler ways to get done.

I won't spend much time on these simple positive developments, important as they were. Many scholarly tasks have become much easier to do, and they simplify getting our scholarly work done. Everyone will have their own list of these benefits. Here's my list of what's made my work easier, and others may have somewhat different lists. Most younger scholars don't really know how hard we worked in the old days!

Finding What You Want to Read

When I started graduate work in 1946, I could only read past and present issues of the few sociological journals then being published by going to the main reading room of the University of Chicago's Harper Library, where bound volumes of the *American Journal of Sociology* (*AJS*), the *American Sociological Review*, and *Social Forces* (which made up most of the serious sociological literature at that time) waited for me. This was serious because the *AJS* was then the only place I had access to translations, for instance, of classics like Georg Simmel's essay "The Secret and the Secret Society," the kinds of things that inspired our daydreams about the kind of work we might ourselves one day produce. If I wanted to have a copy of my very own to read at my leisure, to ponder over, all I could do was what I actually did do: copy it out by hand. And I did that, and so did my fellow students. Which was, not long afterward, made unnecessary by the spread of copying machines, in turn eventually replaced by online archives which, eventually, my new computer let me read whenever I wanted via the internet. And I didn't even have to have access to a major university library to enjoy this access. My local branch (North Beach) of the San Francisco Public Library can get most of what I need for me and deliver it to my home computer.

If you think this wasn't such a big problem, remember that I could read these journals because I was a student at one of the premier universities in the country, which had a famous and much envied library, where such materials were easily available. Many other students had it less easy. To have an idea of the deprivations others suffered, you can read the lengthy sections Umberto Eco (2015, 45–105) devoted to these troubles in his book addressed to students preparing to write the thesis required from anyone wanting a complete (with all the bells and whistles) Italian bachelor's degree. He fills many pages with advice on which specific libraries, in which Italian cities (smaller cities were more deprived than bigger ones with major universities) not only had relatively complete runs of important periodicals, and ample holdings of government documents and other items possibly relevant to their topics, but also the collections of esoteric manuscripts, letters, and other personal papers and printed materials so important for historical and literary research—information now relatively easily available via a simple online search. A related simplification, researchers studying historical questions can now more and more easily find online time series for many collections of routine statistics going back to the initiation of such data-gathering. A small example: Richard Howe told me how short a time it took him to locate a pretty esoteric (to me, anyway) historical fact: the number of real estate firms operating in New York City over more than a century, a fact tangential to *Material City*, his large and detailed study of the building and rebuilding of that city since the first settling by Europeans in the seventeenth century:

> It took [me] less than an hour to get to the sources for annual data on the number of real estate firms operating in New York City for most of the years between 1784 and 1915, but then I already had, from previous researches, a pretty good idea of where on the net I might find this data—it's kind of like getting to know a really enormous library, perhaps very daunting at first, and with many pitfalls, but gradually you get to know, so to speak, the "shape" of the collection, and it all gets easier and faster after that. In this case it was easy enough because I already knew that the internet archive (https://archive.org) had scans of a great many 19th century city directories that list all (or a great many) of the businesses operating in the city: lumberyards, real estate agents, blacksmiths, grocers, accountants, and so on—it helps that the scans of most of these source documents are searchable.

Bibliography

Much of our scientific and scholarly work requires us to manage some bibliographic references, so that we can easily and accurately provide our readers with complete information on the articles in scholarly journals and the scholarly books we refer to in what we write. The classical way of doing this was to write all the information for each item on a file card, and then file those cards alphabetically by authors' last names. Of course, physical mishaps could occur and all that work would be lost. Or the cat would knock the box over and you'd have to sort them again. Far worse, special approved formats existed then (and still do) for such bibliographic information, different formats for different kinds of items: books, journals, government publications, etc. Some of it was quite arcane, and various journals and publishers have different formats for the same items. Confronted with this situation, strong folks sometimes just cried. (If you don't believe me, read Eco's lengthy discussions of proper formats for bibliographical items scattered references throughout the text.)

No more. Computer programs (take your pick, there are several) do the job for you. With the item to be recorded in front of you, you fill in the blanks for items like author, title, publisher and place, and date of publication, etc.; tell the program what standard publication format you're trying to satisfy, and it will format the entries appropriately. When you make the bibliography at the end of what you're writing, the program will arrange all the citations alphabetically for you,

We all hope that the articles and books we write will be published by scholarly journals and publishing houses. All of these publication outlets have style books, and they don't always agree on the proper form for these references. There is, of course, the MLA (Modern Language Association) version, but for me the more relevant one has always been what the *AJS* required. But now, with my references safely stored in a full-featured bibliographical program, I'm ready for either one (or anything else that might be required of me). I just pick the publication outlet I'm aiming for, and the computer does the rest.

Arranging Ideas into an Argument
Your research and work in the library have given you, as you intended they should, a lot of ideas, a lot of points about which you can write more or less authoritatively. You intend them to stand in relation to each other in such a way that they will convince your readers to accept whatever observations and con-

clusions you have arrived at, and hope to do that by arranging them so that it will be clear that *this* item is the conclusion you've reached and *these* other items support your conclusion, in fact make it unassailable.

But, of course, ideas and random thoughts don't arrange themselves into arguments, even when you feel that a logical arrangement lurks among them, *is there*, even if you don't know what it is at the moment. But, now, when there's a problem, someone will make an application that helps us deal with it. So many designers decided that they could make an idea arranger, a program that would let you assemble more-or-less random thoughts into a coherent outline. Just as people wrote computer code to do statistical analyses, which used to take a lot of time because you had to do them by hand with a small office calcula-tor, but now can be done by the machine while you refill your cof-fee cup. And so word processors began to include idea handlers. You created small text units and could then move them around on the screen, arranging and rearranging them and in that way found the "best" way to get what you had in mind made into intelligible larger units which functioned as simple outlines of the helter-skelter ideas your mind had come up with. There was almost no friction in redoing a whole intellectual apparatus— after all, you were just rearranging lines of type! But with a little patience and perseverance you could find an arrangement that revealed a pattern of connections, and that in turn led to a crude first draft of those random thoughts and you were on your way. These programs were often called *outliners* and that's one way to think of them that's familiar to many writers. (Andrew Abbott has written a comprehensive and invaluable guide to the more mundane uses and pitfalls of working in an environment shaped by computing and all its sequelae and explained how to use them efficiently in *Digital Paper* (2014). No need to repeat that here.)

CITATION ANALYSIS

Computers have entered so deeply into the fabric of scholarly work that we don't have far to look to find the current embodiment of C. Wright Mills's insight that *personal problems* of milieu are the personal and private side of *public issues* of social structure. The new machines solved some organizational and individual problems for some actors but also created new ones for others who had not had those difficulties before. Technological developments have produced a lot of new problems for academic writers, but I'm going to focus on just one of them: citation analysis.

People who work for a living usually find themselves judged, to some degree, by their output: the work they do, the actions they complete, the objects they produce, and by their rate of output, the quality of what they produce, and whatever else might be deemed of interest. For those of us in the teaching and writing trades—professors, other teachers, researchers, and authors—these measures usually include some combination of classes taught, numbers of students taught, the success of their students (in whatever way that might be measured), and other activities that are part of whatever teaching they do. Sometimes university administrations evaluate members of their staff by the size of the research grants they bring to the university's bank account.

But for many of us in this line of work, the major measurement of success is usually *publication*: the number and quality of written products—reports of research and thinking done and published in appropriate (usually what are described as "peer-reviewed") journals, and in books. Getting an academic job depends to some extent on the number of books you've published as well as the number of articles you've published in reputable journals in the relevant field, journals which publish articles judged worthy by scholarly peers, people known to be competent to judge, hence the common adjective "peer-reviewed." Other indices may be taken into account, of course, but there is usually no public record of the criteria administrators and others rely on to evaluate scholarly productivity.

Such indices give the people who make these fateful judgments ways to make them without resorting to such once common and accepted methods as asking trusted friends in the field for their private judgments of people, or relying on the judgments of a faculty committee whose members might not be eager to read a pile of books and papers they aren't really interested in (I speak from personal experience). Institutions avoid these alternatives for fear of being criticized (or even sued) if they use less formal methods that might be shaped by racial, gender, or other forms of bias. University administrators, in particular, want a basis of judgment everyone will accept as non-discriminatory, something as above criticism as the methods contemporary symphony orchestras use to audition candidates for positions by having them play behind a screen, which makes visible characteristics like gender and race unavailable as criteria. As a result, accusations of such bias in orchestra hiring are no longer tenable.

So methods that require busy faculty members to read large amounts of printed material about topics that may well not interest them don't really do the job. What better criterion is available? Well, you could count *how much* people produced!

But what could you count that would satisfy that inevitably fuzzy requirement? An article published in a journal that presented itself as scholarly or scientific, that's what. There it is: an object of attested-to quality no one can quarrel with. You can see it and feel it. You can't easily dismiss it as mere opinion, because scientific peers, experts in the field, with a right to speak authoritatively, have said "Whoever wrote this knows what they're talking about. When you count this, you're counting real accomplishment. You can settle scientific arguments about scholarly quality with this number."

That seemed better: an unequivocal number, a real number you could tie to an easily identified and socially/professionally accepted physical entity, a number you could do arithmetic operations like addition and subtraction with ("how many articles?" isn't ambiguous or a matter of judgment and allows simple and unarguable comparisons) and have people accept the results as real enough to settle arguments. Such a number would let faculty or administrators choosing between candidates for jobs or promotions make judgments of scholarly achievement that no one could dismiss as "mere opinion," debatable, and so unable to settle disputes.

But counting the number of publications was just baby steps. Because yes, you could count how many articles Professor X published, but what you really wanted to know was more likely something more subtle and difficult to measure: Professor X's reputation in the field: ordinary, not so good, a star? That requires a more sensitive measure. How about the number of times the article is cited in other people's articles? After all, people wouldn't cite an article if it wasn't good in some unambiguous way.

Now we're getting somewhere! And computer technology makes it simple to increase the ease of counting such things without increasing costs. So why not make a person's "citation count" a standard criterion of judgment? And that's what has happened, "naturally."

Of course, it's not quite that simple. I might, after all, cite your article as an example of a stupid idea everyone should reject. Or to remind readers that although Professor X's article had showed this result, Professor Y had uncovered a flaw in the experiment that nullified X's world-shaking conclusion. Happens all the time.

Nevertheless, a complex edifice of organizational thinking and administrative practice has grown up around the possibilities opened up by counting citations. You want to know how good a scholar is? Count the number of publications. Which of two scholars (professors, candidates for a faculty position or promotion, etc.) is better? Compare the number of publications, yes, but then add the number of citations and take the one who has more. And there's at least one more layer: the "impact factor" of the journals in which scholars have published. Who has published more in journals that are cited more often by other scholars? Not to mention the increasing interest in counting mentions of a scholar's publications in social media. . . . All of which will be enough to sufficiently impress any academic official (and especially those ignorant of the field of knowledge in question) to settle the question.

However. . . . This is where Campbell's Law (Donald Campbell 1979) creates a highly relevant obstacle to any such simple solution. Here is the complete statement of Campbell's wonderful insight:

> The more any quantitative social indicator is used for social decision-making, the more subject it will be to corruption pressures and the more apt it will be to distort and corrupt the social processes it is intended to monitor.

Simple and elegant, and the proof is everywhere.

Campbell, originally an experimental psychologist and trained in experimental method as was customary in his field, soon realized that true experiments could not be done in any of the social sciences because no one would let social scientists treat human beings the way laboratory scientists treated rats and other experimental animals. You couldn't manipulate people that way, because they were free enough to reinterpret the conditions of any experiment and because the institutions where experiments were done were sensitive to the public relations, if not always the moral, issues involved. In fact, there were so many impediments to doing real experiments that Campbell and his colleagues (Shadish, Cook, and Campbell 2001 is the latest version) devised a number of compromises—they called them "quasi-experimental designs"—which relaxed one or more of the conditions required for a true experiment and explained how each deviation from the complete model limited the scope of your conclusions.

Campbell and his colleagues, working in the 1960s (the years of social experimentation that came with Lyndon Johnson's Great Society programs), soon saw how the logic of social experimentation could be applied to the evaluation of specific social programs, by varying the quasi-experimental interventions among the various organizations and communities targeted by those programs. Campbell's experiences doing the kind of "evaluation research" those programs required forced him to recognize the phenomenon he immortalized in Campbell's Law (quoted above). An experimenter might choose a condition for the social program to be tested, but the subjects of the experiments—organizations and the people responsible for them—inevitably and quickly understood how the numbers their actions piled up could be used in ways that might help or hurt their interests. And so, just as routinely, did their best to make sure that the numbers came out the way that gave the best outcome for them, manipulating them in ways their organizational positions and knowledge made available to them. Who knew better how to do that? And that's been a robust finding. It's what people controlling organizations do, if they can (and usually they can).

The application to the case of citation counts is straightforward. People who know (or even suspect) that they may be evaluated with such a measure will try to raise their citation count. I didn't know how to do that nor did I care, being long past the age when such measures could affect anything important to me.

But, in 2003, I learned about an oddity in one of the important journals in sociology, the *American Sociological Review*, which bore directly on this issue. Charles Camic, at the time coeditor of the *ASR*, asked me to comment on a phenomenon he thought he had noticed—the increasing length of the titles of articles submitted to the journal. He sent me a list of the titles of all the articles submitted to the journal during the previous year, and I wrote a short research note (Becker 2003b). He published it and I reproduce it here.

LONG-TERM CHANGES IN THE CHARACTER OF THE SOCIOLOGICAL DISCIPLINE: A Note on the Length of Titles of Articles Submitted to the *American Sociological Review* during the Year 2002

Have the titles of sociological articles increased in length in recent years? And, if they have, how can such a change be interpreted? This analysis is based a list of the titles of all the articles submitted to the American Sociological Review during the calendar year 2002.

The list occupied many pages and I didn't actually count all the articles, but I did count the number of titles on one page and multiplied that by the number of pages of titles I had before me, and concluded that there were roughly a thousand (a number of titles occupied more than one line, the number varying from page to page, which made this short-cut slightly suspect). I counted the number of words in the first 100 titles and can thus provide some simple statistics (there's no reason to think that the first four pages were any different than the rest, since the titles were not arranged in alphabetical order). The average length of a title based on this sample of 100 (10%) is 11.7. The median is 11, indicating that the distribution is not weird in some of the ways it might have been. The range is large, the shortest titles having only 4 words while the longest had 23.

There are no comparative data from earlier years to test the hypothesis that titles are getting longer. What generated interest in the length of titles was the intuition that there had been a decline in short titles which contained a complete idea in a few words. Goffman's "On Cooling the Mark Out" is an example of a concise, informative title, of a kind many people think they no longer see and wished they did. And I could think of others from that far back in the discipline's history, and so can anyone else who has ever taken a Ph.D. exam: "Social Structure and Anomie"; "Good People and Dirty Work"; "Conditions of Successful Degradation Ceremonies"; "Co-operation and Competition in a Bureaucracy"; "Some Remarks on Typological Procedures in Social Research"; "The Social Integration of Peers and Queers"; "On the Relation Between Individual and Collective Properties"; "Ecological Correlations and the Behavior of Individuals"; and so on.

I can only speculate about why authors are getting wordier in identifying their work. But I can use the list of titles of articles submitted to the ASR to describe what authorial practices make titles so noticeably longer than they once were.

1. Colons appear very frequently (15 out of 21 titles on a haphazardly selected page had titles consisting of two phrases separated by a colon). The phrases they separate differ considerably, but very often (I'm not going to bother with any more statistics, take my word for it when I say something happens a lot) they consist of two versions of the same idea, one a little more general than the other, one more catchy, the other more sober, factual, and scientific-sounding. Other colon-ized titles consist of an abstract proposition or concept, followed by an historical or geographical or organizational specification of the particular data used to explore or test the more general idea. (I give no examples, but readers can easily verify these observations in any issue of the ASR, AJS, or other journal in the field).

2. Many titles (I think I could say most) list variables, sometimes two, sometimes three or four, rarely more. The variables are often displayed in a causal relationship, indicating that A "determines" or "influences" or has an "impact" on B. Sometimes the title consists of the names of A and B, as in: "A and B," or "A. B, and C." In some cases, the list of variables is linked to a temporal or geographic specifier, as in "A, B. and C in 19th Century Paraguay" (this title is my invention). The more elements of the research plan and argument included in the title, the longer the title, naturally.

3. Titles often refer to the methods used to gather data or to analyze it, as in "an ethnographic study of X" or the naming of a particular statistical technique. Or they specify the data source used: a Census, a collection of historical materials, or official documents (e.g., police or school records).

What I make of these observations is that authors are trying to get more and more of their article into the title so that a casual reader, flipping through a journal and not even stopping to read the abstracts, will see what the article is about and will be able to determine whether to look further. Authors create a title that tells you whether their article will fit into any of the convenient slots in contemporary sociological practice for which we use the shorthand phrase "the literature." I can look at the title and see whether the article deals with "my" theoretical problem, "my" area of the world, "my" specialty niche and topic. If it does I can figuratively turn the corner of the page down and come back later to see if the article could be useful to me. Or maybe not bother with that nicety and just cite it in a parenthesis or footnote.

To give these notes a little historical depth, and make up for the lack of data for other time periods, I'm going to rely on my memory of conditions in sociology when I first got into the business around 1950. I began reading "the journals" in the late 40s and published my first article the year I received my Ph.D. (1951). At that time, there were essentially two "major" journals (*ASR* and *AJS*), one semi-major journal (*Social Forces*), and a number of smaller journals that weren't widely read. Some of these latter were regional journals, others were subject matter specialty journals, but there weren't a lot of them. A number of journals in other fields occasionally published work of sociological interest (*Psychiatry* published Goffman as well as classic studies of mental hospital organization by Morris Schwartz). Demographic and criminological journals published some material of interest to the field, as did the *Journal of the American Statistical Association*. Few sociology books that weren't textbooks were published. The publication of a serious book was an event for everyone.

The relatively small amount of publication had an obvious cause—the relatively small number of sociologists compared to today (I think there were about a thousand professional sociologists in 1950)—and an obvious consequence, which was that everyone pretty much read everything. "Keeping up with the literature" was not the chore it's since become. There were no computerized literature searches, and no one needed them. A reasonably energetic reader knew, without any strain, what was going on. Not just in your own neck of the woods, but in the field generally.

Which meant that if Goffman or Merton or Hughes or Duncan or almost anybody you could name published an article with a title whose meaning wasn't obvious, sociologists had an idea what the piece was about and, if they didn't, would probably read it anyway.

The comparison I'm proposing suggests that today's authors, members of a much larger authorial class than 1950's, worry that they won't be read at all (Bruno Latour has explained that the biggest hurdle any author faces is not to be criticized or misquoted but not to be noticed at all). So they use the title of their article to advertise to the passing reader that they have something here that you want: Look at my variables! Look at my concept! Look at my historical period! Look at my data! Not knowing what the passing reader might be looking for, the best strategy is to put everything that might be of interest in the title, just in case. Why not?

And there's good reason to play the game this way. Remember that the administrators who decide on tenure and promotion increasingly rely on citation counts to quantify the vague idea of the "reputation" they hope their academic employees will have plenty of. Using the right words in the title might land your article in the output of more literature searches and thus improve your chances.

If this sounds snotty, and I fear it does, the snottiness is not aimed at the authors who pursue such strategies but at the administrators who make them necessary. If anyone, including me, hoped that the result of this exercise would be some magic solution to the problem of the increasingly formulaic character of journal articles, as exemplified in their increasingly lengthy titles, I have surely disappointed them.

But it can't be helped. Organizational realities don't give way easily to tricks that might be discovered by the kind of cursory investigation undertaken here.

What I had was really less a finding than a hunch. But James Moody (2006) checked the results from my absurdly small sample of articles over a longer period and concluded that my conclusions about the length of titles and the use of colons in them remained true when tested against the complete population of articles, as found in all titles in the *ASR* from 1963 to 1999 and all titles indexed in *Sociological Abstracts* for the same time period. He found that the length of titles had indeed increased substantially over that period, as had the use of colons in titles. And, alas for authors, this practice had turned out to be magical thinking. Here's Moody's final judgment: "*These data suggest no relation between the* number of words in the title and achieved visibility. The coefficient for citations never approaches statistical significance and is negative, not positive. These findings suggest that long titles are not effectively capturing reader's attention." In other words, solid evidence triumphs over the wishful thinking of anxious (or maybe just cynical) authors.

So the coming of the computers has been a mixed blessing.

10 : A Final Word

Reading this book will not solve all your writing problems. It will hardly solve any of them. No book, no author, no expert—no one else can solve your problems. They are yours. You have to get rid of them.

But you might get some ideas about how to solve them (or at least start working on them), from things I've said. You can, for instance, avoid the curse of trying to get it right the first time, and so not doing it at all, by writing anything that comes into your head, an Anne Lamott style shitty first draft. You know, if you've followed my arguments (and hers), that you can clean it up later and therefore don't have to worry about the first draft's sure-to-be-there flaws.

You can avoid the wooliness and pretentiousness of "classy" writing by going over your prose repeatedly, taking out words that aren't doing any work. You can think about what kind of person you want to be in your writing and how the persona you adopt will affect the credibility of what you say for the audience you want to reach. You can take your metaphors seriously and see if they say still makes sense. By simply paying attention, you can get a lot of what you do under control.

I could keep on, in this fashion, summarizing what I've already said. But you can pick out these tips as easily as I can. Knowing the tips won't, as I said, solve the problems. None of this will work unless you make it your habitual practice. To get the good of these or any other tips, use them, try them out in a variety of circumstances on a variety of writing chores. Adapt them to your preferences, style, subject matter, and audience. You have read them, but they're still mine. Until you make them yours by using them, reading about them is just another way of evading the hard work of changing your ways.

The preceding suggests that will power and hard work will take care of matters. Although I've tried to avoid it, that Ben Franklin moral has lurked in everything I've said. It's partly sound: nothing will happen without the work. It's misleading if it leads you to think that working hard is all it takes. Many sociologists work very hard but accomplish little. You also have to take some chances, let others see your work, open yourself to criticism. That may be frightening, even painful, in the short run. But the long-range consequences of not getting your work done are much more painful.

Writing anything—letters, journal entries, memoranda—will take some of the mystery and danger out of writing. I write a lot of emails. I also write memos, to myself and to people I work with or share some interest with. I look through these random, barely censored documents for ideas, half-stated but possibly interesting, maybe even the beginnings of something more serious.

A second lesson of this book, implicit in every chapter and explicit in most of them, is that writing is an organizational act, done in response to whatever constraints, opportunities, or incentives the organization you write in presents to you. So another reason these tips might not improve your writing is that the social organization you work in demands bad writing. Sociologists and other scholars often insist to me that they could not get their work accepted by professors, editors, and publishers if it were written in the plain style I've advocated. (See Hummel and Foster's letter to the editor about chapter 1, quoted earlier.) I don't believe that's generally true, but it certainly might be true at times and in some organizations. George Orwell believed that the pressure to disguise political realities led officials and their supporters to write in a way that disguised reality rather than communicating knowledge about it. Some people think that scholars operate under similar constraints, perhaps not political, just built into the working assumptions of disciplines. A friend who is a psychologist once told me of being congratulated on a somewhat unconventional paper by the editor of a major journal, who immediately added, "For God's sake, don't send it to me. I wouldn't dare to print it, because it's not in the right form!"

If social organization causes problems, it also contains the materials for solutions. Scholars shouldn't assume, for instance, that they must do things in an inferior way without making some tests. The discipline may contain the organizational resources you need to do things differently. You can find out if you really have to write badly by trying something else and seeing what happens.

Social organization may, in still another way, keep you from making these (typically) simple and safe experiments. The patterned activities of scholarly life often hide the social supports that allow you to take chances. Indeed, as Pamela Richards made clear in describing the risks of writing, scholars often actively undermine each other. You can't take any of the chances I suggest, modest as they are, if you have good reason to fear your colleagues, junior and senior. You can avoid that by actively building networks of mutual help. As Richards also says, if you try you can find those helpful people, you can take risks and check out your fears, discarding those you can overcome.

Some people have thought my suggestions for seemingly endless rewriting unrealistic or needlessly heroic. No one has that much time, they say. How can you stand to work so hard? That shows a great misunderstanding. No one has done the careful studies that would prove it, but I'm convinced that scholars who write as I've suggested take less time to do seven or eight drafts than other people spend on one. They have no special gift. It's just the difference between trying to get it right in your head the first time and then, and only then, doing it on paper or a computer monitor and fixing up little things as you go along. Nor are such writers unusually able to bear anxiety. Instead of bearing it, they avoid it by first doing only what is easy to do and moving in small steps from that to something marginally harder. The easier cleaning-up steps reduce the punch of the real anxiety producers.

Finally, apply sociology's great liberating message to your own scholarly situation. Understand that the troubles you may have are not entirely your own doing, not the result of some terrible personal defect, but something built in to the organization of academic life. Then you will not add to the trouble by blaming yourself for what you haven't done.

So the moral, Pollyannaish as it sounds, is Try It! As a friend once said to me, the worst that can happen is that people will think you're a jerk. It could be worse.

DEFINITELY THE LAST WORDS

Since I concluded the first edition of this book on that note, I've gotten older, I retired from teaching, and have had less to do with organized academic life and so don't have the same kind of immersion in the culture of academia. But I don't like the way things have gone. I used to tell myself, when I first became a sociologist, that if teaching and research got to be too much trouble, I could always go back to playing the piano in bars for a living. After a while that was just tough talk. I couldn't go back to that life, even if I'd wanted to, because it had disappeared. The places I imagined I could play in had traded in their small bands for a big TV, people who had dances and parties hired rock bands, and the jobbing environment I thought I could depend on were pretty much gone. Sociology turned out to be a far better business to be in, and I've never regretted switching.

But I'm glad my professorial career took place when it did. I had taken care to be born in a year that led me to begin teaching in 1965, when the number of students entering college increased beyond what any administrator had anticipated. (Why didn't they see it coming? Demographers had told them this baby boom generation was on its way.) Universities and colleges suddenly needed teachers, and needed them in a hurry. I had been contentedly living the life of a "research bum," paid to do research and publish it rather than teach. All my friends felt sorry for me, because I didn't have an academic job, but when the boom hit, I had published two books and quite a few articles (what else did I have to do?) and was a very saleable commodity, suddenly in demand as a professor.

College enrollments had soared. So had the number of students taking sociology classes and the number of books that could be sold to them. The number of graduate students preparing to teach all those undergraduates also increased, as did the market for the research monographs they read as part of their training and then taught to their own students. There were always a lot of jobs in this academic boomtown.

As the number of sociologists increased, so did the number of sociological organizations and journals representing different specialties and theoretical positions (see the discussion in Becker and Rau 1992). Publication was never a problem. With all those new journals looking for articles, sociologists of every tendency, both the famous and the not yet famous, found outlets for their work. Young authors found a welcoming environment for their books too, as new publishers began to compete for manuscripts, not just in sociology but in all the social sciences.

Every young person in graduate school in the new millennium eventually realizes that it's not like that anymore. Jobs are hard to come by. Publishing, whose main function had been to let people know the latest research and thinking in a field, acquired the new and unwelcome responsibility of serving as a major part of the apparatus universities used to choose who they wanted to hire, who they wanted to promote and give tenure to, and what they wanted to pay them. You got a job, especially a "good" one, and got promoted by publishing, especially in what the consensus had settled on as the "best" journals.

As the quantity of your publications assumed crucial career importance, professors (especially those lower down on the ladder) rushed to get more and more articles into print. And soon that wasn't enough. There were so many articles—how could you judge which ones were reliable indicators of the excellence you sought? So faculties increasingly relied on citation counts and journal impact factors to make crucial personnel decisions. Publishing the resulting very large number of journals, and selling them to (mainly university) libraries, had become a big business mostly monopolized by a few giant companies.

The competition for scarce space, especially in the "major" journals given special weight by promotion and tenure committees and deans, became ferocious. The resulting large numbers of submissions forced editors to use impersonal bureaucratic procedures for judging contributions (Abbott 1999, 138–92, tells the sad story), as journals increasingly insisted on rigidly formulaic presentations. Scholars in vulnerable career stages, quite reasonably, mostly choose to play it safe, and write articles that have the major features of what they see around them.

These features are nowhere officially decreed. They arrived at their status as "what everyone does" naturally, through the recommendations of multiple referees and a circular process in which authors looked at the journals to see what a proper article looked like and imitated it, so that articles arrived on the editor's desk with these characteristics already in place. (In a sad perversion of the job, referees sometimes made their complex and ritualistic criticisms in an effort to further their own reputations as up-to-the-minute and reliable scholars.)

I decided to make a small experiment. I wanted to test the idea that the social organizations sociologists worked in had become substantially less open to variations in ways of presenting data and writing about what those data mean, much more insistent on standard formats and formulae than they had ever been (which had been bad enough). I made a small investigation, a variant of the experiment conducted by Anthony Trollope, the well-known nineteenth-century British novelist, who submitted a story (using a pseudonym) to a British review which had previously happily published his work, as a sort of experiment on the effects of fame on editorial judgment. He didn't do as well with the pseudonym as with his own more famous name; the editor returned his story with a note that encouraged him to keep trying (Trollope 1947, 169–72). He concluded, as he was entitled to, that reputation influenced editorial judgment.

I intended my variation of Trollope's test to see whether the editorial judgments in sociology had become as rigid as I feared, whether there really was such an insistence on standardized formulaic solutions to the problems of presenting data and ideas, resulting in the increasingly unreadable content so many people had begun to complain of. A friend, the editor of a major journal, didn't believe things were as bad as I claimed (and, you'll remember, as the critics of the first chapter of this book claimed too, when I still didn't believe it). At his suggestion, I submitted an article to his journal.

I had published, in France and in French (Becker 2001), an article about Erving Goffman's stylistic solution to the problem of the biases that infect our work when we use the conventional language of social life, as exemplified in *Asylums* (Goffman 1961). I thought it was a nice piece, not earthshaking but useful, as did the editors of the book it had appeared in. My friend, the editor, thought it would do, and sent it to three referees. But this didn't replicate Trollope's experiment as well as we had hoped. I did not hide my personal knowledge of Goffman (we had been graduate students together at the University of Chicago in the 1940s and 1950s) and the referees easily guessed that I was the author. The many personal references made that obvious. And I was testing a different idea: not that the author's name and reputation made no difference, but that, despite those things, and the overall favorable judgment I somewhat immodestly expected, the grip of contemporary practice would not allow the publication of the article in the slightly unconventional form it then existed in.

My experiment succeeded where Trollope's had failed. The referees did not surprise me. I wish they had, rejecting it or accepting it on the merits of its ideas and credibility. They thought it was an interesting article by a well-known author which contained some worthwhile ideas. But . . . the piece just didn't "fit" the journal's format, its style, its mission. It didn't—this was a major criticism—refer to the "Goffman literature." And the style was too informal, not sufficiently scholarly and academic. The referees were responding to some well-known tendencies of the supervisory committees and other representatives of sponsoring organizations (in this case an important sociological organization) who sit in judgment on the work of editors and editorial advisory boards. While these overseers do not second-guess every editorial decision, they do respond to (and anticipate) complaints from their constituencies. When an article doesn't do what has become routine to do (like citing dozens of articles from the literature conventionally thought to be relevant to its topic) someone will complain, thinking that these tendencies have acquired the force of quasi-law. Editors learn to avoid those complaints which at the least excite a flurry of bureaucratic correspondence. This self-reinforcing tendency is an enormously conservative force perpetuating many bad editorial practices.

My small experiment demonstrated to me the difficulty even a well-known scholar has trying to publish in the best journals these days without toeing the line on bibliography and stylistic matters. The organization of publication opportunities has changed. What used to be acceptable no longer is. And the new rules have taken on the inevitability of "what everybody knows."

That's a pessimistic conclusion and I have to modify it substantially. I completed the experiment by sending the same article to another journal, *Symbolic Interaction*. (Full disclosure: I was once editor of this journal and it represented what I might have thought of as "my people.") And, as I expected, they accepted and published it (Becker 2003a). A more accurate and less pessimistic conclusion would recognize that, because of the enormous increase in publication outlets I mentioned earlier, you can publish almost any article, if you're willing to publish it elsewhere than in the "flagship journals" of the discipline (a sacrifice I was quite willing to make, since I wasn't looking for a job or promotion or any of the other things that might depend on this specific high-status achievement).

In fact, hardly anyone can publish in those journals anyway. They simply don't publish enough articles in a year to allow very many people that honor. These complementary facts of social organization mean that complaints that "you have to do it that way or else" are only partly true.

Book publishers have traditionally been much more open to stylistic variation. The editors, who do most of the work of finding potential books for them, differ in the audiences and markets they target and in the ambitions and tastes their lists reflect. They look for books that will interest many people, they hope, but especially the audience their previous publications have recruited, people with this or that particular interest. They look, too, for informative books, excellent scholarly work, which are also readable. They rely, just as journal editors do, on people in the field to tell them whether the work meets standards of good research and scholarship. They want their publications to bring honor to their house and make some money, or at least break even. The committees that oversee the work of academic publishers don't represent the specialized interests and fads of one particular field. Book publication, as a result, is more diverse, open to more variation than journals, with different sponsors to satisfy, can abide.

Deans who rely on lists of the "two top journals" in each discipline to guide their personnel decisions generally do not work from formal lists of the top book publishers. And, while everyone in a field has an informal idea of the relative ranking of book publishers and would prefer to be published by "the best," books (no matter who publishes them) count for a lot in hiring and promotion decisions, so authors who find an adventurous publisher (and there are many) can take more chances with stylistic variety. Publishers typically care less about the niceties of academic punctilio and more about pleasing readers. As a result, books provide an outlet for material that doesn't fit the requirements of a standard journal format any better than my article on Goffman did. (My Goffman article, in fact, now appears as Chapter 13 in Becker 2007.)

But the same "what everybody does" problem has crept in here, too. A friend who I know has my best interests at heart told me that I really had to start my book on evidence (Becker 2017) with a roadmap to its contents, a list of the topics that it would take up in the chapters to come. For instance: "Chapter 2 presents the theory relevant to this research. Chapter 3 describes the methods I used to gather the data . . . ," and so on. When I asked him (and others who have impressed on me the necessity of organizing my book that way) why I should subject my readers to such a recitation, he explained that if I provided that guide and organized the book's contents accordingly, these potential readers would be able to find just the thing they're looking for, without having to engage in a laborious search, implying that of course no one would read a whole book all the way through on the off chance that there might be something of use to them in it. I've explained to these well-meaning friends that I try to start my books with a story or a set of facts that presents readers with a puzzle that should interest a sociologist to such a degree that they will continue to read to find out how I propose to solve it for them. They shake their heads sorrowfully, indicating that that isn't how people read books these days.

Finally, though, online publication is opening new possibilities every day, allowing you to create your own article or book and make it available to the world without a traditional publisher. Self-publication doesn't carry the warrant of quality that publication in a peer-reviewed journal, or by a prestigious publishing house, does. But many readers have already concluded that peer-reviewed journals don't deliver the quality or interest that the guarantee of peer review promises either. Some quite different ways of distributing what we think we know are already here. We just haven't yet realized their full utility. That task, and the task of analyzing the data on these changes, I leave to a new generation of scholars.

References

Abbott, Andrew. 1999. *Department and Discipline: Chicago Sociology at One Hundred*. Chicago: University of Chicago Press.

———. 2014. *Digital Paper: A Manual for Research and Writing with Library and Internet Materials*. Chicago: University of Chicago Press.

Antin, David. 1976. *Talking at the Boundaries*. New York: New Directions.

Arendt, Hannah. 1969. Introduction. *Walter Benjamin: 1892–1940*. In Walter Benjamin, *Illuminations*, 1–59. New York: Schocken.

Bazerman, Charles. 1981. "What Written Knowledge Does: Three Examples of Academic Discourse." *Philosophy of the Social Sciences* 11, no. 3 (September): 361–87.

Becker, Howard S. 1967. "History, Culture and Subjective Experience: An Exploration of the Social Bases of Drug-Induced Experiences." *Journal of Health and Social Behavior* 8 (September): 163–76.

———. 1974. "Consciousness, Power and Drug Effects." *Journal of Psychedelic Drugs* 6, no. 1.

———. 1980 [1951]. *Role and Career Problems of the Chicago School Teacher*. New York: Arno Press.

———. 1982a. *Art Worlds*. Berkeley: University of California Press.

———. 1982b. "Inside State Street: Photographs of Building Interiors by Kathleen Collins." *Chicago History* 11 (Summer): 89–103.

———. 2001. "La politique de la présentation Goffman et les institutions totales." In *Erving Goffman et les institutions totales*, edited by Charles Amourous and Alain Blanc. Paris: L'Harmattan.

———. 2003a. "The Politics of Presentation: Goffman and Total Institutions." *Symbolic Interaction* 26 (4): 659–69.

———. 2003b. "Long-Term Changes in the Character of the Sociological Discipline: A Short Note on the Length of Titles of Articles Submitted to the *American Sociological Review* during the Year 2000." *American Sociological Review* 68: iii–v.

———. 2007. *Telling about Society*. Chicago: University of Chicago Press.

———. 2014. *What about Mozart? What about Murder? Reasoning from Cases*. Chicago: University of Chicago Press.

———. 2017. *Evidence*. Chicago: University of Chicago Press.

———. 2018. *Outsiders: Studies in the Sociology of Deviance*. Glencoe: Free Press.

Becker, Howard S., and James Carper. 1956a. "The Elements of Identification with an Occupation." *American Sociological Review* 21 (June): 341–48.

———. 1956b. "The Development of Identification with an Occupation."
   American Journal of Sociology 61 (January): 289–98.

Becker, Howard S., and Robert R. Faulkner. 2006a. "Le répertoire de jazz."
   In *Énonciation artistique et socialité*, edited by Jean-Philippe Uzel, 243–48.
   Paris: L'Harmattan.

———. 2006b. "'Do You Know . . . ?' The Jazz Repertoire: An Overview."
   Sociologie de l'art.

Becker, Howard S., Blanche Geer, and Everett C. Hughes. 1968. *Making
   the Grade: The Academic Side of College Life.* New York: John Wiley and
   Sons, Inc.

Becker, Howard S., Blanche Geer, Everett C. Hughes, and Anselm L. Strauss.
   1961. *Boys in White: Student Culture in Medical School.* Chicago: University
   of Chicago Press.

Becker, Howard S., and William C. Rau. 1992. "Sociology in the Nineties."
   Society 30:70–74.

Berger, Bennett. 1981. *The Survival of a Counterculture: Ideological Work and
   Everyday Life among Rural Communards.* Berkeley: University of California
   Press.

Bernstein, Theodore. 1965. *The Careful Writer: A Modern Guide to English
   Usage.* New York: Atheneum.

Booth, Wayne. 1979. *Critical Understanding: The Powers and Limits of
   Pluralism.* Chicago: University of Chicago Press.

Bulmer, Martin. 1984. *The Chicago School of Sociology: Institutionalization,
   Diversity, and the Rise of Sociological Research.* Chicago: University of
   Chicago Press.

Campbell, Donald T. 1979. "Assessing the Impact of Planned Social Change."
   Evaluation and Program Planning. 2, no. 1: 67–90.

Campbell, Paul Newell, 1975. "The *Personae* of Scientific Discourse." *Quarterly
   Journal of Speech* 61 (December): 391–405.

Carey, James T. 1975. *Sociology and Public Affairs: The Chicago School.* Beverly
   Hills, CA: Sage.

Chapoulie, Jean-Michel. 2001. *La tradition sociologique de Chicago 1892–1961.*
   Paris: Seuil.

Clifford, James. 1983. "On Anthropological Authority." *Representations* 1
   (Spring): 118–46.

Davis, Murray S. 1971. "That's Interesting! Towards a Phenomenology of
   Sociology and a Sociology of Phenomenology." *Philosophy of the Social
   Sciences* 1: 309–44.

Eco, Umberto. 2015. *How to Write a Thesis.* Cambridge, MA: MIT Press.

Elbow, Peter. 1981. *Writing with Power: Techniques for Mastering the Writing
   Process.* New York: Oxford University Press.

Faris, Robert E. L. 1967. *Chicago Sociology: 1920–1932*. San Francisco: Chandler.

Faulkner, Robert R., and Howard S. Becker. 2009. *Do You Know . . . ? The Jazz Repertoire in Action*. Chicago: University of Chicago Press.

Fine, Gary Alan. 1995. *A Second Chicago School? The Development of a Postwar American Sociology*. Chicago: University of Chicago Press.

Fischer, David Hackett. 1970. *Historians' Fallacies*. New York: Harper and Row.

Flower, Linda. 1979. "Writer-Based Prose: A Cognitive Basis for Problems in Writing." *College English* 41 (September): 19–37.

Flower, Linda, and John Hayes. 1981. "A Cognitive Process Theory of Writing." *College Composition and Communication* 32 (December): 365–87.

Follet, Wilson. 1966. *Modern American Usage: A Guide*. Edited by Jacques Barzun. New York: Hill and Wang.

Fowler, H. W. 1965. *A Dictionary of Modern English*. 2nd ed. Edited by Ernest Gowers. New York: Oxford University Press.

Garfinkel, Harold. 1967. *Studies in Ethnomethodology*. Englewood Cliffs, NJ: Prentice-Hall.

Geertz, Clifford. 1983. "Slide Show: Evans-Pritchard's African Transparencies." *Raritan* 3 (Fall): 62–80.

Gerth, H. H. and C. Wright Mills, eds. 1946. *From Max Weber: Essays in Sociology*. New York: Oxford University Press.

Goffman, Erving. 1952. "On Cooling the Mark Out: Some Aspects of Adaptation to Failure." *Psychiatry* 15 (November): 451–63.

———. 1961. *Asylums*. Garden City, NY: Doubleday.

Gowers, Sir Ernest. 1954. *The Complete Plain Words*. Baltimore: Penguin.

Gusfield, Joseph. 1981. *The Culture of Public Problems: Drinking-Driving and the Symbolic Order*. Chicago: University of Chicago Press.

Hughes, Everett C. 1971. "Dilemmas and Contradictions of Status." In *The Sociological Eye: Selected Papers*, 141–50. Chicago: Aldine.

Hummel, Richard C., and Gary S. Foster. 1984. "Reflections on Freshman English and Becker's Memoirs." *Sociological Quarterly* 25 (Summer): 429–31.

Kidder, Tracy. 1981. *The Soul of a New Machine*. Boston: Little, Brown and Company.

Kuhn, Thomas. 1970. *The Structure of Scientific Revolutions*. 2nd ed. Chicago: University of Chicago Press.

Lakoff, George, and Mark Johnson. 1980. *Metaphors We Live By*. Chicago: University of Chicago Press.

Lamott, Anne. 1994. *Bird by Bird: Some Instructions on Writing and Life*. New York: Random House.

Latour, Bruno. 1983. "Give Me a Laboratory and I Will Raise the World."
In *Science Observed: Perspectives on the Social Study of Science*, edited by
Karin D. Knorr-Cetina and Michael Mulkay, 141–70. Beverly Hills, CA:
Sage.

———. 1984. *Les microbes: Guerre et paix*. Paris: A. M. Métailié.

Latour, Bruno, and Françoise Bastide. 1983. "Essai de science-fabrication:
Mise en evidence experimentale du processus de construction de la
réalité par l'application de méthodes socio-semiotiques aux textes
scientifiques." *Études françaises* 19 (Fall): 111–33.

Latour, Bruno, and Steve Woolgar. 1979. *Laboratory Life: The Social
Construction of Scientific Facts*. Beverly Hills, CA: Sage.

Malinowski, Bronislaw. 1948. *Magic, Science and Religion and Other Essays*.
Garden City, NY: Doubleday & Company.

McCloskey, Donald N. 1983. "The Rhetoric of Economics." *Journal of Economic
Literature* 21 (June): 481–517.

———. n. d. "The Problem of Audience in Historical Economics: Rhetorical
Thoughts on a Text by Robert Fogel." Unpublished paper.

Merton, Robert K. 1972. "Sociology, Jargon, and Slangish." In *Sociology:
Theories in Conflict*, edited by R. Serge Denisoff, 52–58. Belmont, CA:
Wadsworth.

Mills, C. Wright. 1940. "Situated Actions and Vocabularies of Motive."
American Sociological Review 5: 904–13.

———. 1959. *The Sociological Imagination*. New York: Oxford University Press.

Moody, James. 2006. "Trends in Sociology Titles" *American Sociologist* 37, no.
1: 77–80.

Moulin, Raymonde. 1967. *Le marché de la peinture en france*. Paris: Éditions de
Minuit.

Orwell, George. 1954. "Politics and the English Language." In *A Collection of
Essays*, 162–77. Garden City, NY: Doubleday.

Perlis, Vivian. 1974. *Charles Ives Remembered: An Oral History*. New Haven,
CT: Yale University Press.

Platt, Jennifer. 1996. *A History of Sociological Research Methods in America*.
Cambridge: Cambridge University Press.

Polya, George. 1954. "Mathematics and Plausible Reasoning." Vol. 2, *Patterns
of Plausible Inference*. Princeton, NJ: Princeton University Press.

Rains, Prudence Mors. 1971. *Becoming an Unwed Mother*. Chicago: Aldine.

Rose, Mike. 1983. "Rigid Rules, Inflexible Plans, and the Stifling of
Language: A Cognitive Analysis of Writer's Block: *College Composition and
Communication* 34 (December): 389–401.

Rosenthal, Robert. 1966. *Experimenter Effects in Behavioral Research*. New
York: Appleton-Century-Crofts.

Schultz, John. 1982. *Writing from Start to Finish*. Upper Montclair, NJ: Boynton/Cook Publishers.

Selvin, Hanan C., and Everett K. Wilson. 1984. "On Sharpening Sociologists' Prose." *Sociological Quarterly* 25 (Spring): 205–22.

Shadis William, Thomas D. Cook, and Donald T. Campbell. 2001. *Experimental and Quasi-Experimental Designs for Generalized Causal Inference*. Stamford, CT: Wadsworth.

Shaughnessy, Mina P. 1977. *Errors and Expectations: A Guide for the Teacher of Basic Writing*. New York: Oxford University Press.

Shaw, Harry. 1975. *Dictionary of Problem Words and Expressions*. New York: McGraw-Hill.

Simmel, Georg. 1950. *The Sociology of Georg Simmel*. Translated by Kurt Wolff. Glencoe: Free Press.

Stinchcombe, Arthur L. 1978. *Theoretical Methods in Social History*. New York: Academic Press.

———. 1982. "Should Sociologists Forget Their Fathers and Mothers?" *American Sociologist* 17, no. 1 (February): 2–11.

Strunk, William, Jr., and E. B. White. 1959. *The Elements of Style*. New York: Macmillan.

Sutherland, J. A. 1976. *Victorian Novelists and Publishers*. Chicago: University of Chicago Press.

Trollope, Anthony. 1947. *An Autobiography*. Berkeley: University of California Press.

Waller, Willard. 1932. *Sociology of Teaching*. New York: John Wiley and Sons.

Weber, Max. 1946. *From Max Weber: Essays in Sociology*. Translated and edited by H. H. Gerth and C. Wright Mills. New York: Oxford University Press.

Whyte, William Foote. 1943. *Street Corner Society*. Chicago: University of Chicago Press.

Williams, Joseph M. 1981. *Style: Ten Lessons in Clarity and Grace*. Glenview, IL: Scott, Foresman.

Zinsser, William. 1980. *On Writing Well: An Informal Guide to Writing Nonfiction*. New York: Harper and Row.

Index

Carper, James, 27, 84
Cattell, Raymond, 137
causality, 8, 45, 54, 73–74, 134, 151
censoring, 12, 156
Chapoulie, Jean-Michel, 86
Charlton, Joy, 51
Chicago school of sociology, 86–90, 124
Chicago Seven, 86
citations: computer analysis of, 143–54; count of, 147, 149, 153, 160; employment and, 159–60
classics, sociological, 102, 125–27, 131–32, 141
classy writing, 28–33, 36, 98, 155
Clifford, James, 32
code words, 35
coherence, 10, 16, 18, 86, 134, 144
colons, 151, 154
computers: arranging arguments and, 143–44; beginnings of, 137–39; benefits of, ix, 55–56, 140–54; bibliographies and, 142–43; changes in routine tasks and, 139–54; citation analysis and, 143–54; "cut and paste" with, 39, 140; drafts and, 144, 155, 158; formats and, 143; getting it out the door and, 110–11, 113; ILLIAC, 137; increasing title lengths and, 149–54; journal searches and, 140–42; Kidder on, 110; large-scale computing and, 138; as mixed blessing, 154; organization and, 145; outlines and, 55, 144; personal, 138; professionalism and, 146, 152; revising and, 140; style and, 140, 143; trusting, 71; word processors and, 55, 71, 144; writing habits and, 91–94
confidence, ix, 10–11, 60, 105, 107–8

contact sheets, 95
content, 74
Cook, Thomas D., 148
"Counter-Establishment R&D" (Becker and Dedijer), 94
creativity, 61–62, 124–25, 128, 139
criticism, 1, 5; confidence and, 11; differences in, 36; drafts and, 11, 17, 21, 81, 86, 94, 103; editing and, 65, 81; English composition and, 8–9; literature issues and, 124, 132, 162; professionalism and, 86, 90, 94–95; readers and, 40; referees and, 160; responding to, 8, 21–22, 146, 153, 156; risk and, 103, 107
"cut and paste," 39, 140

deadlines, 18, 89, 95, 118–19
Dedijer, Steven, 94
Dickens, Charles, 119
diction, vii
dissertations, viii, 10, 50, 98–99, 114, 128, 131
drafts: challenges of getting started and, 44; computers and, 144, 155, 158; criticism and, 11, 17, 21, 81, 86, 94, 103; editing and, 66, 68, 73, 81; English composition and, 5, 10–13, 16–22; final, 22, 95; first, 11, 18, 22, 44, 50, 83, 95, 103–4, 144, 155; getting it right the first time and, 40–42; Lamott on, 12–13, 50; One Right Way and, 44, 49–51; outlines and, 10, 13, 15; perfectionism and, 20; professionalism and, 83–86, 92–96; risk and, 99–101, 103–4, 106; rough, 12, 16, 20, 92, 99; second, 5, 94; third, 94; unplanned, 51; writing habits and, 10, 18, 85, 95

and, 7–9, 129–30; editing and, 65–68, 72, 78; English composition and, 12, 15–17, 21; literature issues and, 123, 127, 129–31; narrative, 121; One Right Way and, 51, 53; organizational, 42; professionalism and, 87–90

Theory of Justice, A (Rawls), 114

thesis writing, 24, 45, 50–54, 83–84, 91, 141

Times Literary Supplement, 30

tone, 6, 16, 24, 32, 80–81, 85

Trollope, Anthony, 96, 119, 161–62

trust: author-reader, 20; class experiments and, 11; computers and, 71; editing and, 17; friends' advice and, 105–6, 112, 146; getting it out the door and, 112; risk and, 103–7

Unfinished Woman, An (Hellman), 101

University of Chicago, 83, 86, 97, 141, 161

Velho, Gilberto, 9

Vienna Circle, 8

vocabulary of motives, 115–16

Waller, Willard, 132–33

Walton, John, 35–36

Warner, W. Lloyd, 45

Watts Towers, 96

Way, Brenda, 37

Weber, Max, 15, 54, 124, 126–27, 131–32

Weiner, Lee, 85–86

Weston, Edward, 97

White, E. B., 29

Whyte, William Foote, 33, 91

Williams, Joseph M., 29, 41, 76

Windows, 138

Wirth, Louis, 86, 124

Wittgentstein, Ludwig, 34

Woolgar, Steve, 33

word processors, 55, 71, 144

writing habits: anxiety and, 4, 86, 90, 120–22, 158; barrage of knowledge and, 31–32; computers and, 91–94, 139–54; creativity and, 61–62, 125, 139; doing easiest tasks first and, 55; drafts and, 10, 18, 85, 95; grade concerns and, 40–42; increasing title lengths and, 149–54; isolation and, 19–20, 112, 128; journals and, 38; literature issues and, 123–36; perfectionism and, 20 (*see also* perfectionism); placeholders and, 7; professionalism and, 91–96; rewriting and, 6; routines and, 2–5, 95; scientists and, 33; solidification of, 10, 18; tips for, 156; worrying over rules and, 13–14

Yankel, Chaim, 124, 126